PRESTON
MURDERS AND
MISDEMEANOURS

KEITH JOHNSON

AMBERLEY

First published 2020

Amberley Publishing
The Hill, Stroud
Gloucestershire, GL5 4EP

www.amberley-books.com

British Library Cataloguing in Publication Data.
A catalogue record for this book is available from the British Library.

ISBN 978 1 4456 9662 1 (print)
ISBN 978 1 4456 9663 8 (ebook)

Typesetting by Aura Technology and Software Services, India.
Printed in Great Britain.

CONTENTS

FOREWORD BY MIKE HILL

Every day the most gripping of real-life stories are played out in front of judge and jury as justice is served. Murder, robbery, kidnap, con tricks and all kinds of wrongdoings capture the intrigue of those going about their everyday life.

It has been this way for centuries when the guilty and the innocent learn their fate, pay their penance or walk free with their name cleared and head held high. Murderers sent to the gallows to pay for their crimes alongside those poor souls wrongly convicted of someone else's foul deeds. At the other end of the criminal scale history recalls others who found themselves deported to faraway lands as punishment for offences that a modern-day criminal would receive barely a slap on the wrist for.

As Keith is a local historian of great repute it is little surprise to learn of his fascination with the tales of Lancashire's courts. His popular Chilling True Tales series of books often drew upon details from the courtroom to lift the lid on some of the county's most jaw-dropping and macabre stories from down the ages.

Many of the true tales Keith has unearthed for this, his latest book come from the pages of more than 130 years of the *Lancashire Post*. To this day the newspaper still has a reporter in court every day taking notes and relaying the daily goings on in the county's courts. It is a central pillar of what papers are all about, acting as the eyes and ears of the public so justice is not only done but is seen to be done.

Such was the treasure trove of long-lost stories Keith would find on his regular trawl through the local newspaper archives he started writing them up and submitting them to the *Post* for a new audience to pore over. These old crimes have proved so popular with readers during the last decade that we created a dedicated home for them in the newspaper. Consequently, each week through his Court Archive we dip in and out of the public gallery to reveal all manner of stories, shedding light on crimes and criminals who had long since faded from popular memory.

In recent years many readers have contacted the *Lancashire Post* asking if Keith had a book available from which they could devour more of these often salacious tales. At last their prayers have been answered with *Preston Murders and Misdemeanours*. Here Keith has assembled some of his personal favourite tales together for the very first time. Take a journey through Lancashire's legal history with Keith by your side; there is no better guide.

Mike Hill, Communities Editor of
the *Lancashire Post*

INTRODUCTION

This collection of tales will transport you back through the annals of murder and misdemeanours in Preston and the neighbourhood. It chronicles events that occupied the courts and brought criminals to justice while looking back at mishaps and misfortune that befell local folk.

Judges and justices, coroners and court clerks, barristers and briefs all played their part from times when justice was swift and often delivered harshly with unflinching retribution; the poacher, the pickpocket, the prostitute and the pilfering thief all brought forward to account for their crimes, whether petty or paramount.

Robbery with violence, murder and manslaughter were often committed by those who had evil in mind in the days when they faced the threat of hangman's noose, or being sentenced to a life of penal servitude, or even being transported across the seas to a foreign shore.

There were days when the cotton masters ruled and had their feasts while others toiled in famished times, the harsh justice served reflecting the master's desire to maintain control. Poverty and pestilence amid the working classes were often breeding grounds for immoral behaviour and rouges and ruffians were commonplace.

Villainy, knavery, harlotry and thievery, as described by one Victorian scribe, is suggestive of a town that was out of control and full of undesirable people. In reality it was only the fact that they had to live amid squalor and strife that led most onto the path of lawlessness. Reflecting on those days it is apparent that the alehouses and the gin palaces had to accept their share of the blame. Many of the crimes committed were carried out by those in liquor, who, once they sobered up, realised the folly of their behaviour.

As the population rapidly increased so did the police force, and with strict discipline in their ranks, dealt not only with robbers, thieves and vicious thugs, but street brawls and riotous behaviour that stretched their resources.

These tales tell of those people who were murdered, poisoned, mistreated or cheated and they deserve our sympathy. It is apparent that those who handed out the punishments had duty in mind and the judges were unflinching in doing so. Indeed, we should not be critical of the verdicts delivered, but admire a system of justice that attempted to be fair. Neither should we view those criminals too harshly, but consider the circumstances in which they were driven to commit often dreadful deeds.

Read on and you will encounter the apple thieves, the railway robbers, the coin forger, the sweetheart slayer, the bigamist, crimes of passion and other tales that were compelling reading in their time and can be recalled today, in more enlightened times, with thought-provoking sentiment.

RURAL COMMUNITY LIVING IN FEAR

In the early part of the nineteenth century, as many people left their rural surroundings to seek employment in the towns and cities, many country folk felt isolated. By this time Preston was feeling the effects of the introduction of the cotton trade and a mid-eighteenth-century population of around 5,500 had doubled in size.

It was a time when the laws of the land were very strict and no place in the country was more foreboding than Lancaster Castle, home of the twice-yearly Lancaster Assizes. In late November 1803 word reached Preston of a robbery in the hamlet of Oakenclough, within Bleasdale, at Fell House.

It was home to brothers Thomas and John Eccles, both over sixty years old, and an elderly housekeeper and a young servant girl. Shortly after midnight on the 29 November, the two brothers were suddenly alarmed by three men making their way upstairs and into their bedroom. All had blackened faces and wore handkerchiefs tied across their features. They had with them a lighted candle, a pistol and a wooden club a yard long.

They threatened the brothers and demanded £20, saying they had a payment to make. Thomas was lying on the near side of the bed and one of the intruders attempted to tie his hands. He resisted and was struck three or four violent blows to the head. One of the intruders then brandished the pistol, threatening to shoot both brothers, who then held out their hands to be bound. After securing the brothers to the bed the intruders went into the next room and bound the two servants together.

When they returned to the main bedroom John Eccles told them they should have the £20, but they replied they would take it themselves and began to break open a desk. From inside the desk they took over £200 in gold guineas and bank notes. Leaving the brothers tied, they then went into the cellar and from a chest took several silk handkerchiefs, smelling bottles, a few silver coins and various trinkets. Having satisfied themselves, they fastened the doors on the outside and went away, leaving all the inhabitants tied.

In the days that followed it was learnt that the robbers had, prior to the theft, been seen in the White Horse at Myerscough and that Richard Eccles, who lived in Preston, a cousin of the victims, had been drinking in town in their company a couple of days prior to the crime. Suspecting he was a planner of the robbery he was arrested at a foundry in Preston and taken into custody at the house of correction.

It was believed the perpetrators of the robbery hailed from Manchester and Mr Nadin, the deputy constable of that place, became involved. Information was received there that a man called Jonas Clark had been seen drinking in a public house, swaggering with a purse of gold, and on being apprehended he was identified as a culprit.

The next evening James Chadwick was taken up for smashing a shop window and stealing some articles. Being brought before the magistrates, he was suspected by Mr Nadin as being involved in the robbery at Oakenclough.

A search the next day of Richard Eccles' house in Preston led to the discovery of a letter some three weeks old from a man called Henry Barker, saying he had arrived safe in Manchester and that he would call again in a fortnight. When this was communicated to Mr Nadin the suspect Barker was immediately arrested. In the possession of all three had been found a considerable number of gold coins and several of the articles that had been stolen. Consequently, all three men were transferred to Lancaster Castle to await the Lent Assizes.

Richard Eccles, Henry Barker, James Chadwick and Jonas Clark would spend over three months incarcerated until their trial took place. With over thirty-six prisoners to be brought to justice, it was said that Lancaster Castle presented a melancholy picture, being a black barometer of the vicious state of the country.

The trial took place before Mr Justice Chambre and it was learnt that Jonas Clark had in the meantime opted to turn king's evidence. His testimony was enough for guilty verdicts to be returned against Henry Barker and James Chadwick, but not enough to convict Richard Eccles.

Above left: His Lordship Sir Giles Rooke reprieved the resident executioner Edward Barlow.

Above right: Joseph Nadin, deputy constable of Manchester, had a ruthless reputation.

Both Clark and Eccles were at once allowed to walk free, while the convicted pair had to wait overnight to learn their fate. Next morning they got little sympathy from the learned judge, being informed that they were sentenced to death. In all, thirteen received sentence of death at that assizes, although before he left Lancaster Castle, His Lordship announced that all but three had been reprieved and would be given lesser sentences.

Left to their fate were Barker, Chadwick and Joseph Brown, who was convicted of highway robbery. On the last Saturday of April 1804 the unfortunates Barker, aged thirty-eight, and Chadwick, aged twenty-seven, were executed on 'The Drop' behind the castle by resident executioner Edward Barlow. A week later Brown suffered the same fate.

Two years later Edward 'Old Ned' Barlow found himself facing the same fate as those he had executed. Convicted for stealing a gelding, he was sentenced to hang, but earned a reprieve from His Lordship Sir Giles Rooke, who handed him a ten-year prison sentence within the Lancaster Castle walls. It meant, having already executed upwards of seventy of those condemned in the previous twenty years, he was free to continue his unpleasant work while serving his sentence. Besides carrying out public executions Edward Barlow was always on hand to administer floggings to many convicted felons.

This pattern of trial and conviction for a whole range of crimes besides murder was carried out until a change of the law in the mid-1820s, with horse stealing costing a couple of men their lives and a conviction for bestiality earning three others a date with the executioner. Add a handful of highway robbers, a dozen men guilty of uttering forged notes, four rapists and a burglar or two and it was common to see anything from five to ten men being hung at Lancaster each year.

TO LANCASTER AND A GALLOWS FATE

In mid-February 1806 Christopher Simpson, aged twenty-three, was up before the Preston magistrates accused of assaulting and robbing Stephen Sparrow on the king's highway, in the township of Claughton. After considering the evidence the chairman Samuel Horrocks, the MP for Preston, ordered him to be sent to Lancaster Castle to await his trial for highway robbery.

Already being held at Lancaster was Mary Jackson, aged twenty, who had at the October 1805 assizes been cleared of the murder of Ann Smith of Manchester, but still held in custody awaiting trial for felony. Jackson had come to the attention of Preston folk in June 1805 when a gentleman living on the outskirts of town had employed her as a dairy maid. She had stayed in his employment about a week when he had cause to visit the Preston market. When he returned she had absconded having robbed the house of linen, wearing apparel, silver teaspoons and around £5 in cash. On being missed she was pursued and overtaken at Haslingden where she delivered up the whole of the articles she had stolen, and was, from mistaken leniency, allowed to go away.

However, justice was soon to overtake her for on the Sunday morning following she was apprehended in Church Street, Manchester, being suspected of the murder of Ann Smith. A billboard had been offering a £30 reward for her apprehension. When arrested, she had in her possession a bundle containing silk gowns and other articles of female wearing apparel, of considerable value, which she was strongly suspected of stealing at Bolton, from where she had just arrived. A pawnbroker's ticket was also found upon her, which was for a watch that had belonged to Ann Smith.

At her assizes trial the evidence against Mary Jackson seemed strong, but she implicated a man named as James Cheetham, who she claimed had given her the articles belonging to the deceased. The doubts led to the jury finding her not guilty of murder but subsequently indictments were brought against her for stealing property belonging to Ann Smith and to the suspected theft from Bolton and she was remanded into custody.

Both Simpson and Jackson stood on trial at the assizes in March 1806 before Sir Giles Rooke and both were found guilty as charged, His Lordship sentencing both of them to be executed. In the days that followed both made voluntary confessions of their crime with the hope of salvation when they were despatched into eternity.

Mary Jackson confessed to not only the crime of stealing but admitted murdering Ann Smith and declared that her previous allegations against James Cheetham were untrue. Simpson, who had retained a certain amount of mystery about him, revealed that he had escaped from gaol in Hereford, while under sentence of death for stealing,

Above: Edward 'Ned' Barlow, the reprieved executioner, carried on his gruesome occupation.

Right: The crowds flocked to Lancaster from an early hour to witness the public executions.

prior to arriving in Lancashire and committing the robbery he was convicted for. He also stated that he had in his time broken open fifty houses, stolen over thirty horses, and to have committed more highway robberies than his memory could recall.

Along with a man named James Foxcroft from Manchester, convicted of burglary, the pair were hanged outside Lancaster Castle on the third Saturday of April 1806. A large crowd gathered in the neighbourhood to watch the grim spectacle unfold as the wretched culprits shared the gallows. The death of Edward Barlow, aged sixty-six, within the walls of Lancaster Castle was announced in the *Lancaster Gazette* in mid-December 1812, bringing to an end his notorious career.

THE UNFORTUNATE DEATH OF JOSEPH ROBINSON

On the last Tuesday of February 1821 an inquest was held at the Town Hall before Thomas Miller, the mayor and coroner of Preston, following the death of Joseph Robinson, a mechanic in the employ of Horrockses & Co.

It appeared, from the depositions of the witnesses examined, that the deceased was returning from Clayton Green in company with William Burges on the previous Saturday evening. When they got to Penwortham, nearly opposite two cottages belonging to Peter Horrocks, they were assaulted by three men. Robinson and Burges immediately fled towards the cottages, and while the latter called out for a gun, the former received a violent blow on the forehead from a stone thrown by one of the assailants, William Sharples, aged twenty-nine, who later admitted the act. Robinson immediately called out that he was killed and fell upon the ground. The assailants then ran away and Robinson was taken into the cottage, where his head was bandaged, and shortly afterwards he was able to proceed to Preston.

Robinson and Burgess went forward to Preston with two men accompanying them to the Spread Eagle on Lune Street, where they treated the pair to some ale. Robinson later proceeded to his own home on Fylde Road. On Sunday, although he felt much pain, no apprehension was entertained of serious consequences, but in the night he was taken suddenly ill and died before morning.

The unfortunate Robinson, who had lost his life by this wanton outrage, was known as a quiet, industrious person, and he left behind a wife and five small children, whose sole dependence was upon his labour. The court heard that the Mayor of Preston had set a subscription to relieve, in some degree, the distress of his unhappy widow and children.

The inquest jury, under all circumstances, were induced to limit their verdict to a charge of manslaughter, although it was felt to be a case of a very aggravated nature.

Sharples, having surrendered himself, was committed to Lancaster Castle to await his trial at the Lancaster Assizes in early April. These took place before Mr Justice Best and there was a heavy calendar of crime for the grand jury to consider. They found a true bill against Sharples and the common jury found him guilty as charged. He was then informed that he would be kept in prison for a period of twelve months.

As the assizes drew to a close he was able to reflect on his good fortune as two of his fellow convicts ended the assizes upon the gallows. The hangings of Abraham Wade, aged sixty-seven, and John Quinn, aged forty-six, for uttering forged bank notes took place in mid-April. A number of others who had been sentenced to death for offences such as horse stealing, sheep stealing and burglary had their sentences commuted to transportation across the seas for the rest of their natural lives. All no doubt relieved not to be facing the hangman's noose.

Above left: The victim was attacked on his way back to Preston along the country lanes.

Above right: Robinson had worked in the engine room at Horrockses.

Below: An inquest took place at the Town Hall before Thomas Miller, Mayor of Preston.

ATTEMPTED MURDER OF SAMUEL HORROCKS MP

Early in April 1823 Samuel Horrocks, MP for Preston and co-founder of the Horrockses cotton empire, received an anonymous letter bearing a Manchester postmark at his Lark Hill residence. The writer threatened the life of the former Mayor of Preston if he did not advance the wages and improve the conditions of the Preston cotton workers in line with those in Manchester. It was a threat that Horrocks would have done well to heed.

As was his usual custom, on the last Sunday of July 1823, he attended morning service at Preston parish church. On leaving church he strolled down Church Street intending to visit his business partner, Thomas Miller, who lived in Golden Square. As he entered the gateway of Mr Miller's house Horrocks received a violent blow to the back of his head. Turning round he saw a man brandishing a cleaver. The assailant struck again with three or four blows but with quick reflexes Horrocks

The vicious attack took place outside the Golden Square home of Thomas Miller.

took the force of the blows on his arm. The cleaver was then thrown to the floor and the attacker fled away, but a couple of onlookers pursued him and he was apprehended. Samuel Horrocks, a father of eight, was a sturdy character and he soon recovered from his injuries.

In mid-August 1823 Andrew Ryding, aged twenty-two, a former committee man of the Preston Union, appeared at Lancaster Assizes charged with the attempted murder of Samuel Horrocks. The trial begun at nine o'clock in the morning, lasted for over twelve hours, and the court was crowded to suffocation the whole time. Ryding recalled the torment he had suffered when fellow workers at Horrockses had been imprisoned at Preston for striking without notice when their wages were reduced. Having admitted his actions, the defendant's case was built around a plea of insanity – claiming he had lost the sense of reason.

At the end of a long day the jury retired to consider their verdict. Within ten minutes they returned and announced a verdict of 'not guilty' on the grounds of insanity. Alas, there was no walk to freedom for Ryding with His Lordship Justice Bayley announcing that the prisoner would be detained in custody at His Majesty's pleasure to prevent further mischief.

Sam Horrocks was so determined that he would not be freed that he wrote to Sir Robert Peel, the Home Secretary, who assured him that Andrew Ryding would remain safely locked up within Lancaster Castle. Horrocks need not have worried because in mid-June 1825 it was announced that Ryding had died in Lancaster Castle. His early confinement had been marked by fits of violence before his health declined and he was afflicted by dropsy. The inquest verdict given was that he had died due to a 'Visitation of God'. As for Samuel Horrocks, he lived until 1842 when he died aged seventy-six at his Lark Hill home.

PORRIDGE LACED WITH ARSENIC

In the middle of May 1827 news soon spread of the sudden death of John and Mary Scott, who had kept a small provisions shop in Bridge Street, in the Marsh Lane area of Preston. The couple had been taken ill after partaking of porridge cooked by their daughter Jane, aged twenty-one, who was well known as a 'depraved and dissolute character'.

The mother of two illegitimate children, she was taken into custody even before her parents were buried at nearby Trinity Church, and was sent to Lancaster Castle to await her trial at the August Assizes. Initially, she was put on trial for her father's death and despite proof of the purchasing of arsenic, which she claimed was to poison rats, and evidence of her bragging that soon 'she would be inheriting her parents wealth' the Jury returned a 'not guilty' verdict.

She was then given the choice of being tried the next day for her mother's killing, or waiting until the next assizes in March 1828. She chose the latter and after a further six months locked away in the dungeons she appeared in court in a weak and sickly state. This time the jury found her guilty with a plea for mercy, but Baron Hullock had no hesitation in announcing that a sobbing Jane Scott would be executed within the week.

Many people from Preston set off in the early hours to witness the hanging on the third Saturday of March 1828. During her last hours she admitted her crimes and in a pitiful state she had to be carried to the gallows.

The parents of killer Jane Scott were buried in the churchyard of Trinity Church.

APPLE SCRUMPERS UP BEFORE THE MAYOR

It appears that in the summer of 1828 apples were plentiful and much sought after in Preston. So much so that a group of young boys decided to go seeking some in the meadows and fields around Preston. Their expedition led them to the orchards and gardens of the townships of Ingol and Fulwood. With youthful exuberance they plundered the orchards of Mr Webster in Fulwood and then a Mr Reay in Ingol. Not content with their haul, they spied the small cottage home of an elderly widow woman in Ingol. Alas, before they could get their hands on the juicy crop of apples she was waving a broomstick at them and her small but ferocious dog was chasing them away, biting the heel of one of the boys as they scarpered. Word of their expedition reached town and a couple of Chief Constable Thomas Walton's small force of police officers rounded them up.

Consequently, on a Saturday morning in mid-August at the Town Hall seven of them, aged between eleven to fourteen, were up before the formidable Samuel Horrocks, cotton master and magistrate. Their behaviour was viewed seriously and Horrocks expressed his displeasure at their antics. Two of the boys were identified as the ring leaders of the youthful delinquents. For Richard Hewitt and Richard Brakell the punishment was severe, with the former being sentenced to six months in the house of correction and the latter receiving a two-month sentence. As for the rest of the accused there was a suitable reprimand before they were set free.

Above left: The Preston of 1828 was surrounded by countryside.

Above right: The apple thieves were up before Sam Horrocks MP.

PRESTON RIOTERS AND A RADICAL

Henry 'Orator' Hunt, the controversial radical, won one of the parliamentary seats for Preston in December 1830 after a fierce campaign beating the Hon. E. G. Stanley, a future Earl of Derby. Wallowing in his victory, Hunt became a familiar figure in the town and often rallied his supporters with stirring speeches and assemblies.

One such occasion in early November 1831 led to riotous behaviour by hundreds of his followers who rampaged through the streets destroying property and threatening the peace of the town. Preston's police chief Thomas Walton and his six constables, aided by militia men, had a torrid time. They, along with the watchmen employed by the cotton mills and factories, attempted to control the mob and restrict their vandalism. Eventually when calm was restored investigations led to the arrest of thirty men, aged between eighteen and thirty.

Windows were smashed at Swainson's cotton mill at Fishwick.

Inset: The followers of Preston MP Henry Hunt went on the rampage.

The lock-up down Turks Head Yard was under siege by rioters.

Inset: The gravestone of Thomas Walton, the first Chief Constable of Preston, is nowadays in the path around the Preston Minster.

Fearing unrest in Preston the magistrates sent the accused to Lancaster Quarter Sessions for trial in January 1832. Witnesses spoke of windows being broken at Swainson's Mill, an arson attempt at Mr Paley's factory, the gates of Grundy's Foundry being smashed, the lock-up in Turks Head Yard being under siege and an attack on the house of correction that was quelled by the military. Numerous incidents occurred leaving townsfolk running for cover as brickbats, stones and boulders were tossed in the air by the flag waving mobs who proclaimed 'Hunt for ever'.

Three days of evidence and identification of the culprits led to ringleaders Roger Walton, John Hodgson, William Dickenson and James Melling being sentenced to eighteen months in prison, with seven others receiving custodial sentences of up to twelve months.

Thomas Walton remained as chief constable until his death in June 1835, aged fifty-one, and he was buried in the family grave at Preston parish church graveyard and his gravestone is now part of the pathway surrounding the present-day Preston Minster.

MARY PORTER AND HER BAND OF JUVENILE THIEVES

In the latter part of 1837 a number of robberies took place in Preston on the Sabbath during the hours of divine service, the thieves taking advantage of entering unoccupied homes while the inhabitants were at prayer. Naturally these opportunist thieves attracted the attention of the recently appointed police chief constable Samuel Bannister and his seven constables.

Through their efforts much progress was made and at the Preston Quarter Sessions in January 1838 a number of young men stood on trial. First up were Edward Eccleston, William Thompson and John Kay, three lads all aged fourteen and diminutive in stature, who were accused of stealing clothing the property of Richard Hogarth in November last. All three pleaded guilty and the court heard they had all been previously convicted of felonies. When each was sentenced to transportation for seven years there were gasps and screams from the public gallery. The same fate of transportation then befell teenagers David Clegg and Henry Salisbury,

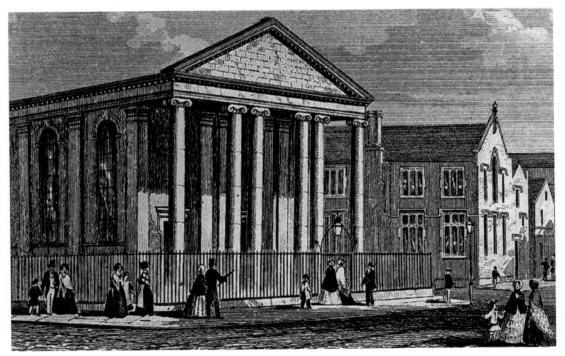

While parishioners gathered for Sunday service at All Saints Church, the thieves struck.

Mary Porter was among those transported to New South Wales.

found guilty of stealing knives the property of a Mr Hargreaves, a crime for which Thomas Clegg, aged twenty-four, was acquitted by the jury.

The police investigations had brought to light the activity of Mary Porter, aged forty-seven, who was charged with stealing a pan from a Mr Sowerbutts and found guilty. At this point Chairman T. B. Addison remarked that for the last fifteen years Porter had been known as a harbourer and trainer of thieves in the town. He then stated that her despicable behaviour had been responsible for the transportation of many young men from Preston, including two of her own sons. Stating that the police had concluded she was behind the gang of Sabbath burglars and had assisted the notorious Clegg gang using her home as a rendezvous for criminals aplenty.

Obviously pleased to have the miserable-looking woman in the dock he informed her that she would follow those she had nurtured in crime and be transported for seven years. By late April she was aboard the John Renwick along with 172 other convicts, arriving in New South Wales, Australia, in late December 1838.

BRUTAL MURDER OF A GANGSMAN

During 1837/38 there was a great influx of Irish labourers into Preston to work on the North Union railway development, including the bridge over the River Ribble. Each group of workers was supervised by a gangsman, who was responsible for paying the men their weekly wages and arranging their accommodation and provisions. One such supervisor was Michael Donohoe, aged forty, who had around twenty labourers in his charge, most living in the Marsh Lane area. Unfortunately, Donohoe's life would come to a tragic end in November 1838 leading to a manhunt and two of the culprits facing trial.

At the Lancaster Assizes of mid-August 1839 James Lackey, aged twenty-nine, and his wife Julia Lackey, aged twenty-one, were charged with the wilful murder of Michael Donohoe in mid-November 1838. Before Mr Justice Coltman the court heard that one of Donohoe's duties each Saturday was to pay his gang for their week's work. In the last week of November, for some inexplicable reason, he did not pay them on the Saturday and it was the following Monday evening before he set about the task. Along with a colleague, he firstly went to the Bay Horse at Penwortham, where he paid four workmen, before proceeding to Brown Street near Marsh Lane, where the bulk of his employees lived.

When Donohoe arrived a dispute arose over an unpaid bill and he refused to pay due wages until Julia Lackey settled the account. A gathering then took place in the house occupied by the Lackey family, where a number of irate labourers vented their fury. Such was the commotion that a neighbour alerted the police and two constables appeared at the house. Things seemed to have gone quiet with Julie Lackey having produced a bill from the local provision shop that indicted she had settled the account.

Not long after the constables departure cries of 'Mercy, murder and robbery' were heard coming from the house. When anxious neighbours tried to enter the premises, the door was bolted. Shortly afterwards all the occupants, except for Donohoe, were seen leaving the house by the back door, which was locked after them as they fled into the night. The police, alerted by the neighbours, arrived back on the scene and after forcing the front door the first sight that greeted them was the lifeless corpse of the ill-fated Donohoe. A mangled and mutilated figure lay on the stone flags awaiting Dr William St Clare when he was called to attend.

The court heard that within hours the Lackey family had fled to Liverpool where James and Julia Lackey were arrested, but other suspects including brothers Patrick and Michael Lackey could not be traced. The pursuit was long but unsuccessful, and consequently just James and his wife stood in the dock at Lancaster Assizes. Although one neighbour testified that through a partly open shutter she had seen both the accused standing over the bloodied body of Donohoe, there was doubt as to who delivered the fatal blows in the bloody skirmish.

As a result the jury saw fit to find the couple guilty of manslaughter and not murder. His Lordship stated that he saw no reason to be merciful and ordered that the couple be transported beyond the seas for life. A tearful Julie Lackey sobbed as she realised she would be parted forever from her young children.

Above: Work began on the original North Union Railway (or German bridge) in 1837.

Below left: A great influx of Irish navvies to work on the railway brought problems.

Below right: Physician William St Clare attended the bloody scene.

STAGECOACH DRIVER IN THE DOCK

In late February 1846 stagecoach driver James Hull appeared at Lancaster Assizes accused of killing and slaying Samuel Rixton Latus by negligent driving on the Preston to Blackburn road in November last. One witness was passenger John Hacking who, seated alongside the accused, stated that the coach was fully loaded with passengers when it left the Red Lion in Preston after five o'clock on a gloomy evening. He testified that the driver had proceeded quickly, both trotting and galloping the horses until they reached Brockholes Brow.

A fully laden stagecoach left the Red Lion on Church Street.

The stagecoach ran away down Brockholes Brow heading for the Half Penny Bridge.

According to him when halfway down the slope there were a number of carts coming up and the horses began to gallop, with the driver attempting to hold them back and then applying the brake. Unfortunately, as they approached the Halfpenny Bridge the coach overturned with the passengers battered and bruised. Hacking's leg was broken in the crash and Latus, who was inside the coach, was the most critically injured, it being necessary to amputate his left leg. Sadly, after lingering for seven weeks he died due to complications.

Another witness, James Clayton, claimed that Hull seemed fresh in liquor and had driven the coach very fast, with it rocking and reeling constantly. The proprietor of the stagecoach, Henry Whalley, was adamant that the prisoner was a good coachman and more than capable of handling the powerful horses used on the day. The problem in his view was that the carts had startled the horses and being fully laden the coach had simply run away. Without much deliberation the jury concluded that no blame was attached to the prisoner and he was immediately discharged.

ELLEN LIKED TO PICK A POCKET OR TWO

On the third Monday of January 1850 four persons, namely Thomas O'Gar, John O'Neil, Ellen O'Neil and John Green, were brought up at the Preston police court charged with picking the pocket of Miss Ann Boys, of Catterall, on the previous Saturday while she visited a draper's shop on Cheapside. Her purse, containing a sovereign and several shillings, along with a watch key, had been taken from her dress pocket while in the store of Messrs Wilson & Lawson. She had been on the premises around fifteen minutes and when she came to pay for her purchases she realised her purse was missing.

Witnesses, including Inspector Rigby, testified Ellen O'Neil, along with Green and O'Gar, being in the shop and standing close to Miss Boys and to John O'Neil loitering outside the premises. After leaving the shop the prisoners made their way to Cannon Street where PC Hindle and other constables arrested them on suspicion of theft. At the police station all the suspects were searched and when O'Gar removed his hat the purse, the watch key, a sovereign and other silver coins were discovered. The others accused had pound notes and silver coins in their pockets. Initially, Ellen O'Neil and John Green gave false identities, but it was eventually discovered that Green was the brother of Ellen O'Neil and that she was the wife of John O'Neil. Claiming they were innocent of the crime, all four were remanded in custody to stand trial at the next Preston Sessions in mid-February.

By the time the trial took place O'Gar, aged eighteen, had entered a guilty plea with the other three facing trial by jury. The evidence submitted suggested that all the accused had been working together on the streets that day indulging in light fingered theft. The jury took little time in delivering a guilty verdict.

Before passing sentence the chairman Mr T. B. Addison remarked that all the prisoners were known to the police as notorious characters. He then revealed that John Green, aged eighteen, had been convicted twelve times, John O'Neil, aged twenty-one, had, since 1844, been imprisoned six times and that his wife Ellen O'Neil, aged seventeen, had four previous convictions.

All the prisoners were then sentenced to seven years transportation, at which point a crowd of female relatives of the prisoners who occupied the front seats of the public gallery commenced yelling and shrieking and making all manner of commotion. Tears and tantrums continued for a few minutes before calm was restored.

While being held at Preston awaiting transportation Ellen O'Neil was visited by a reporter from Manchester who, along with the prison chaplain Revd John Clay, interviewed her. The outcome was a pamphlet entitled 'Extraordinary Confessions of a Female Pickpocket' that recorded her exploits. Born in Stockport, she had, aged fourteen, been influenced by an elder brother who took her to Knot Mill Fair where she watched him stealing purses. Seeing it as easy pickings, she began to follow his example and events such as the Blackburn fair, where she pocketed £3, attracted her. She was soon travelling further afield with other girls and her brothers, being drawn to market days and fairgrounds. A good day in Hull earned her £7 and a festival in York shortly after she wed was fruitful with £12 thieved in a day.

Preston on a Saturday had become a profitable place to visit with £17 taken on one day. Unimpressed by the prospect of a life in the mill, or on the streets as a prostitute as some of her friends, she had chosen thievery, which had on occasions put beer and beef steak on the menu. As the transport ship awaited she had no regrets.

Unfortunately, pickpockets were commonplace in Victorian Preston.

Inset: Prison chaplain Revd John Clay interviewed the convicted woman.

WHEN THE GAROTTE ROBBERS
CAME TO TOWN

In early Victorian days when garotte robbery was rife three such robberies occurred in the neighbourhood of Preston in late 1854. In mid-November Robert Gardner, gamekeeper, was heading back home over old Penwortham Bridge when he was sprung upon by two men who grabbed him by the neck from behind and rifled his pockets. His treasured watch and purse containing twenty shillings being taken as he was thrown to the ground.

Early in December Thomas Byers was walking home to Inglewhite in the early evening and as he neared the two-mile marker on the road to Garstang a man approached him. Suddenly two other men appeared from behind a hedge, grabbed him by the collar and pulling a chain around his throat wrestled him to the ground. Despite kicking out at his attackers he was robbed of his watch, twenty-five shillings and his keys. He was left seriously hurt and bleeding as his attackers fled towards Preston. Later that same night William Holland of Fishwick was robbed by a similar method on Fishwick Brow.

Police intelligence indicated that this gang of thieves were from Liverpool and work by police detectives from the county force led to John Murray, aged twenty-eight, Edward Grogan, aged twenty, and David Tarpy, aged eighteen, appearing at Lancaster Assizes in March 1855 accused of the robberies following arrest in Liverpool. Various witnesses testified as to seeing the men on the nights in question including John Jackson, a shoemaker from Broughton, who saw the culprits near to

Garrotte robbery was rife and caused much anxiety.

the Withy Trees. Both the stolen watches had turned up in Preston and were traced back to Murray, and a lodging housekeeper testified as to their suspicious behaviour. The jury found all three guilty and Mr Justice Parke sentenced them to two months in the house of correction prior to being transported for fourteen years.

Above: The old Penwortham Bridge was close to where the gang struck.

Below: They were sent to the house of correction to await transportation.

A PARCEL OF FISH AND THE MISSING GEMS

Among the respected silversmiths of Preston in 1861 was Mr Lowe of Church Street. One afternoon in mid-February 1861 a man entered his shop asking for a watch key. He was shown a number of keys by Elizabeth Lowe, the proprietor's daughter, eventually choosing one and paying for it. Next he asked to be shown watch chains, lockets, and other trinkets that were on display trays before leaving abruptly. Only when putting the trays away did Miss Lowe realise that a pencil case, a watch, an opal cross and a silver chain had gone missing.

The theft took place on Church Street.

A fishy parcel at the original Theatre Tavern on Fishergate.

That same night two men entered the Theatre Tavern on Fishergate. After buying two glasses of ale one told the landlady he had bought some fish and asked her for some wrapping paper. Making a bundle tied with string, he asked to leave the parcel to be collected later. That night the police were making enquiries into the stolen jewellery and a constable visited the inn. The suspicious drinkers and their parcel came up in conversation. The parcel was opened and among the fish wrapped in tissue paper were the stolen items. Hoping to catch the thieves when they returned, the parcel was sealed up again.

Nothing transpired until the next morning when a woman called to collect the parcel. PC Houghton was on hand to arrest her and eventually two men were arrested. With denials all around it was a complicated affair and only in June did Israel Israel, George Thompson and Mary Wilkinson appear at the Preston Sessions. Israel was accused of the Preston robbery and another in Manchester, Thompson was accused of receiving and a theft in Manchester and the woman charged with receiving. After a four-hour trial the jury found both men guilty, but not the woman. The court heard that both men were habitual criminals and Mr. T. B. Addison sentenced them both to penal servitude for six years. As for Wilkinson she was free to go, but not before getting a warning about her future behaviour.

LEFT BAREFOOTED AT THE OLD DOG INN

It was the custom at the popular Old Dog Inn on Church Street, of eighteenth-century origins, for a servant girl to collect the footwear of any guests and to clean them overnight. On the second Monday of July 1862 four pairs of boots and a pair of bluchers were placed in a row in the kitchen ready for cleaning. Early next morning when the girl came to attend them they had gone missing.

Landlord Thomas Tomlinson had the unenviable task of informing the guests and then informed the police, who immediately circulated information of the theft. Following information received police constable Townley went over to Blackburn the following Thursday where Mary Ann Tout was being held following a tip off from a pawn broker, the woman having been arrested while in possession of all the missing footwear.

She was immediately brought back to Preston to appear at the police court on Friday morning. She claimed that whilst on her way to Blackburn a man had approached her asking her to pledge the stolen articles. She was then remanded in custody until the following Tuesday while further enquiries were made. A couple of pawnbrokers from Blackburn gave evidence as to her conduct, and having a change of heart she admitted the theft. Pleading guilty, she elected to be treated summarily rather than wait for trial. The magistrate Paul Catterall told her that the stolen goods were valued at 30 shillings and that her behaviour had caused much inconvenience. He then sentenced her to three months in prison at Lancaster Castle.

The Old Dog Inn on Church Street, where guests awoke to find their boots were missing.

STEALING MR ANDERTON'S TROUSERS

In mid-November 1864 there were numerous thefts from Preston's public houses. After a number of incidents Thomas Heaps, the landlord of the Shelley Arms in Fishergate, reported to the police that his overcoat had gone missing. The next day Thomas Anderton of the Old Legs of Man reported that his top coat, waistcoat and a pair of trousers had gone missing. Both men gave similar descriptions of the suspected thief.

An overcoat went missing from the Shelley Arms on Fishergate.

Inset: Chairman Thomas Batty Addison.

Clothing was stolen from the Old Legs of Man.

A couple of days later in Blackburn a man was spotted leaving the Adelphi Hotel carrying a coat and a pair of trousers. Aware of the thefts in Preston a local constable followed the man and he was confronted in a urinal close to the hotel with the coat on his back. He was taken into custody and a trunk left by him at the railway station was found to contain numerous articles of clothing stolen recently, mainly in Preston.

In early January 1865 William Prytherley, aged thirty-three, appeared at the Preston Epiphany Quarter Sessions accused of the thefts. At first he stated that a solicitor from Blackburn was to attend to defend him, but when no one appeared he changed his plea to guilty. The chairman Mr T. B. Addison then told the court that the accused was a habitual criminal having been convicted a number of times in London for hotel robberies, including once for 12 months. He was then told that he would spend the next two years imprisoned in Preston's House of Correction. As for the trunk of clothing, some had been reclaimed, but the rest was available for inspection at the police station. Happily, Mr. Anderton had been reunited with his trousers and Mr. Heaps had his overcoat on his back once more.

THE MYSTERY OF FATHER COOPER'S CASH BOX

On the first Sunday of February 1866 the parishioners of St Ignatius Church were aghast when they heard that a cash box, containing £50 and some papers, belonging to Father Cooper had gone missing from the presbytery. The box was discovered over a week later in a room on Walker Street used for scholars, minus the cash, but with the documents intact.

The police took the theft seriously and suspicion fell upon Peter Dewhurst, aged thirty-three, a local handyman who often did work at the church. Within days he was taken into custody. He denied the crime but appeared at the Preston police court where the magistrates ordered him for trial a week later at the next Preston Quarter Sessions accused of theft.

The jury was told he had been in both the church and the schoolroom during the week in question and had the opportunity to carry out the crime. PC Brindle told the court he had seen Dewhurst hurrying along Meadow Street with what could have been the box under his arm on the Sunday evening. A coal merchant, a printer, a surgeon and a couple of publicans were called as witnesses, and they told how he had been busy settling debts and spending freely in the days following the theft, despite previously being hard up.

In his defence it was claimed all the evidence was circumstantial and that he was already in custody when the box was found. After a long day's evidence the jury retired, returning within the hour to announce a 'not guilty' verdict, which was greeted with applause from some parties as Dewhurst walked free.

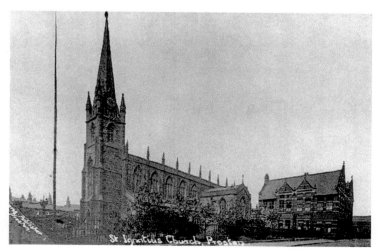

The disappearance of Father Cooper's box caused an uproar at St Ignatius Church on Meadow Street.

A CHILD WAS BORN IN EMMANUEL STREET

During Whitsuntide in 1867 Mary Ann Brandwood, aged thirty-six, a single woman, took up lodgings with Mr and Mrs Eaves in Emmanuel Street, close to where Emmanuel Church was being constructed. Miss Brandwood was a pleasant lodger who worked as a servant and appeared content in her situation. However, she did have a secret that would be revealed on the fourth Wednesday of July.

Emmanuel Church, pictured today, was under construction in 1867.

Inset: Magistrate Thomas Walmsley sent the girl for trial.

Only the corner house of the Emmanuel Street terrace remains.

Unusually, she had spent most of the day before in bed. On the Wednesday Elizabeth Eaves, concerned about her welfare, sent her little girl upstairs to inquire. Brandwood told the child she was unwell and Mrs Eaves took a cup of tea up to her. In mid-afternoon Mrs Eaves went to see her again and Mary Ann told her a weary thing had happened to her. She then revealed that she had given birth that morning and the child was quite dead, it being beside her under the bed clothes. She then asked for a box to put the child in, so that she could take it to the cemetery to be buried.

Shocked by the revelation, Mrs Eaves went to see her sister, Isabelle Brandwood, who lodged in Oxford Street. The pair of them returned with Dr Armiston, who examined the baby, it being a fully grown boy, 22 inches tall. Mary Ann told them the father of the child was John Salthouse, a farmer from Grimsargh, with whom she had been in a relationship for three years. According to her, he had told her to keep her pregnancy close and not let it be known to anyone. Miss Brandwood, who was in a poorly state, was then removed to the workhouse hospital to recover.

She appeared at the Preston police court in early August charged with the murder of her illegitimate child. Dr Armiston believed that the baby had breathed and that the naval string had been cut with blunt scissors. Bruising around the neck made him suspicious of the cause of death. The chairman, Thomas Walmsley, concluded the hearing by ordering the prisoner for trial at the forthcoming Liverpool Assizes.

At the Liverpool Assizes the grand jury ignored the bill charging her with murder and put a charge of concealment of birth in place. It was said that she was a woman of weak intellect and very headstrong in her behaviour. The traumatic events following her pregnancy and her poorly state were mentioned. The jury took little time to return a verdict of not guilty and Mary Ann was told she was free to go.

COURT BATTLE OVER THE HERO HOUND

In July 1876 James Parkinson, a lamp and oil dealer from Church Street, and Thomas Bailey, the landlord of the York Castle public house on Adelphi Street, appeared at the Manchester Assizes over the ownership of a dog called Morgan. This animal of mixed breed – retriever and bloodhound – had in recent times been in the care of a local printer Peter Taylor, who James Parkinson had asked to look after it due to its growing eccentricity.

In April 1876 posters had appeared on hoardings in Preston asking for help regarding the disappearance of seven-year-old Emily Holland in Blackburn. With an £100 reward on offer Taylor volunteered the services of Morgan and the bloodhound was successful in following a trail that led to the discovery of the child's dismembered body concealed up the chimney of a barber's shop in Blackburn. It was evident that attempts had been made to burn the corpse and parts of the trunk and limbs were wrapped up in a back issue of the *Preston Herald* newspaper. William Fish, aged twenty-seven, the owner of the shop had been under suspicion of taking the girl and the discoveries by Morgan led to trial, conviction and execution of him at Kirkdale Gaol.

Back in Preston news of Morgan's part in the solving of the brutal crime led to the great popularity of the animal. There was a tug of war over Morgan's ownership and Bailey claimed that Parkinson had merely been allowed to look after the dog by a third party. Parkinson disputed this saying he had bought the bloodhound for a £1. Bailey told the court that the dog had spent its early years at the public house and that it had been very obedient, fetching his master's hat or handkerchief when called. It was obvious that the dog's fame had made it a commercially attractive animal and after lengthy proceedings the jury declared in favour of Parkinson. Already an offer of £25 per week was on the table for public appearances and one offer had been received of over £200 to gain ownership of the dog that had exposed a savage killer. As for Peter Taylor, a year after the crime he received £100 for his part in the conviction of William Fish.

In the years that followed the trusty bloodhound Morgan continued to be of service to the police. It was used in the search for the stolen body of the Earl of Crawford in December 1881 and in July 1884 it was taken to Middlesbrough to help track down a child killer.

In early July 1886 a fatal accident befell him on Church Street when he was run over by a horse-drawn cab. Morgan, who was eighteen years old, had become quiet deaf in his later years and was oblivious to warning shouts from passers-by. His body was delivered to a local taxidermist.

Above: Morgan the bloodhound smelt trouble for the Blackburn child killer.

Right: Morgan became a much sought-after celebrity.

BLUE BELL INN DAUGHTER SLAIN

The third day of August 1881 was the day that Annie Ratcliffe, aged sixteen, believed she was to marry her lover John Aspinall Simpson, aged twenty-one, at St Paul's Church in Preston. Annie lived at the Olde Blue Bell public house on Church Street, at which place her widowed father was the landlord.

   Although he disapproved of the relationship, Alfred Ratcliffe signed his constant to the nuptials for his pregnant daughter. Annie, dressed in her bridal gown, slipped quietly out of her home early in the morning to rendezvous with Simpson at the nearby Sir Walter Scott Inn prior to the marriage. The couple ordered two glasses of lemonade and went into the bar parlour.

Annie Ratcliffe's wedding day horror.

The Blue Bell Inn on Church Street, a reminder of a terrible tragedy.

What followed led, three months later, to the appearance of Simpson in the dock at the Manchester Assizes accused of the murder of Annie Ratcliffe. Many Preston folk journeyed by rail to Manchester and there was a great rush to claim a seat in the public gallery.

A tearful servant girl from the Sir Walter Scott Inn recalled how upon hearing a scream she had dashed into the parlour to discover a terrifying scene with Miss Ratcliffe, whose throat had been cut by a razor-brandishing Simpson, staggering towards her. The young victim then slumped to the floor and her life expired as she lay in a pool of blood. Simpson remaining seated at the bar table, showing no emotion.

It emerged during the trial that Simpson had not booked the wedding ceremony and gave no reason for his action. In fact, he pleaded 'not guilty' to the capital offence before a crowded court. After two days of deliberations, with many Preston folk called to testify, the jury retired and they returned shortly afterwards with a guilty verdict. It then fell upon Mr Justice Kay to pass sentence of death upon Simpson. So it came to pass that he was executed within Strangeways Gaol towards the end of November 1881 by William Marwood, the public executioner.

A FORLORN SEARCH FOR ANTHONY HENRY

At a Preston Coroner's Inquest Court in September 1883 the jury were told of the death of Paddy McGinty, aged twenty-one, on the first Monday of the month. Evidence was submitted describing a quarrel among a group of harvest workers who were rained off and went to the Baker's Arms public house in Lawson Street to play cards. McGinty and fellow Irishman Anthony Henry were at loggerheads, with the latter storming out of the inn. A few minutes later, as McGinty walked along Lawson Street, he was confronted by Henry, who was brandishing a knife.

Above left: Anthony Henry flees the scene after stabbing Patrick McGinty outside the Baker's Arms.

Above right: Chief Constable Francis Little intensified the search.

Without hesitation Henry struck McGinty a blow on the head and as he fell to the ground his attacker ran from the scene. The incident took place in mid-afternoon, and despite being rushed to the infirmary McGinty was dead by early evening.

The inquest, held before coroner William Gilbertson, was told that Anthony Henry had not been seen since fleeing the scene. He had been traced as far as Meadow Street, down St Ignatius Square, through the school playground and onto Sedgwick Street. There a coachman had refused to give him a lift.

Despite the non-appearance of Henry the jury had no doubt of his guilt, delivering a verdict of wilful murder against the fugitive. Chief Constable Francis Little made sure that the search for Henry intensified and a couple of days later the murder weapon was discovered in the schoolyard ash pit. Baffled by the whereabouts of the accused the police circulated a description of Anthony Henry that included the following: 'he has prominent teeth in his upper jaw and it is with great difficulty that he covers them'. In the days that followed detectives visited many a place where Irish navvies were employed as they attempted to track down the son of an Irish farmer who hailed from County Mayo. Despite the police offering a reward of £100 to anyone who could give information, nothing further was ever heard of the Irishman.

It was a particular disappointment for Chief Constable Francis Little, who had taken control of the Preston borough police force in 1882, at a time when the police force was almost 100 strong and the annual budget, including his £350 salary, was £9,000. Nonetheless, his time as Chief Constable saw many crimes resolved and he led the Preston police force into the twentieth century. Year on year the crime figures were reducing after he took over during troublesome times. Upon his retirement in 1908 much praise was heaped upon him.

A BRUTAL ATTACK LEAVES CONSTABLE CRIPPLED

At the Preston police court in early December 1886 James Leach appeared and pleaded guilty to his part in a brutal assault on PC William Ward of the Preston borough police force a fortnight earlier. The court heard that the constable was on afternoon patrol in the Manchester Road area when he saw a number of men loitering on the corner of Laurel Street. He asked them to move on and they ridiculed his request. Among the group was Leach, who was said to have kicked the policeman, whose head hit a factory wall as he slumped to the ground. A witness of the assault was a woman named Dunnighan, who informed the gathering that the main culprit was a man she knew as Thomas Miller, who had punched the officer in the mouth, knocked his helmet off and attacked him in a brutal manner. Despite a police search Miller had

Above left: The police in Victorian days often faced unruly mobs.

Above right: Alderman Walter Bibby sent Miller to jail.

gone missing the day after the attack, with a warrant being issued for his arrest. For Leach a sentence of one month in gaol with hard labour was delivered.

Not until October 1887 did Thomas Miller appear at the Preston police court after being captured a day earlier in Colne. A strongly built fellow, he pleaded guilty when he appeared in the dock before the mayor, Alderman Walter Bibby. Details of the assault were gone over again and it was said the prisoner was drunk at the time and gave PC Ward a ferocious beating. So vicious had been the assault that the constable had been forced to retire from duty. Besides a fractured jaw, missing teeth and head wounds he had been troubled with severe back pain, being left partially crippled. After seventeen years' service he had been pensioned off on 18 shillings per week unable to fulfil his constable duties.

Dr Pilkington spoke of the suffering that PC Ward had endured and remarked that he had been a strong and powerful man beforehand. Alderman Bibby then informed the court that Miller had eighteen previous convictions including assaults. He then stated it was time to teach brutal people a lesson and sentenced Miller to two years' hard labour.

A CELTIC CROSS FOR ANNIE AND THE SERVANT GIRL

In mid-July 1887 Alfred Sowrey, aged twenty-three, of Stanleyfield Road in Preston, and a pawnbroker's assistant appeared at Lancaster Assizes accused of the killing of Annie Kelly, a nineteen-year-old laundry maid employed at the Bull Hotel on Church Street. The court was told that on the 18 May the pair had gone to the Clarendon Temperance Hotel on Fishergate Hill where Sowrey was said to have taken out a revolver and shot Miss Kelly in the head, before turning the revolver on himself and firing it unsuccessfully. The young Irish lass died within minutes, Sowrey being arrested at the scene.

It emerged that the couple had planned to emigrate to New York, but trouble had flared after Miss Kelly refused to travel until they had been married. Although Sowrey had confessed to the deed, he entered a plea of not guilty, his counsel claiming the revolver had been fired accidentally. The jury recorded a guilty verdict and Mr Justice Day announced a sentence of death upon a distraught Sowrey, who had seemed in an agitated state throughout.

On the first day of August 1887 he was hanged within Lancaster Castle by executioner James Berry. Such was the sympathy expressed for Annie Kelly that almost 2,000 people walked behind her coffin to her grave in Preston Cemetery. A public subscription paid for a magnificent Celtic cross that is inscribed with the words she 'died in defence of her virtue'.

On the first Saturday of December 1887 an inquest took place at the Lane Ends Hotel, Ashton, into the death of Ellen Chamberlain, aged twenty-five, a domestic servant from Ireland. The hearing was told that she had been found in an unconscious state in her room at Helm House in Grosvenor Place, Ashton.

With her employers Mr and Mrs Catterall being away for a few days, the groom Richard Howson had arrived in the morning, but unable to arouse Miss Chamberlain with knocking on the front door and shouting he entered the house through a kitchen window. There was a distinct smell of gas and hurrying to Ellen's room he found the door bolted. He promptly fetched a local constable, and with his aid entered the room through an outside window, finding the room full of gas that was escaping from a switched-on tap. The woman was lying in her bed in an apparent peaceful state and beneath the bed was an equally unconscious dog.

Dr Arminson was immediately called for. He told the jury that he discovered a slight pulse, but, although lingering for another day, the girl eventually died from inhalation of gas that caused congestion of the brain. The coroner observed that a lack of ventilation had been a major contributor to the melancholy tragedy, the jury returning a verdict of accidental death. With her death coming just months after Annie Kelly's tragic killing, she was buried in the same grave, and her passing is recorded on the same Celtic cross.

Above: The inquest into Miss Chamberlain's death took place at the Lane Ends public house.

Right: Alfred Sowrey turns the gun on himself after shooting his sweetheart.

Below: A Celtic cross marks the grave where the two Irish lasses are buried in Preston Cemetery.

CRIME OF PASSION THWARTED BY A CORSET

During the year 1891 Elizabeth Worthington, aged eighteen, lived with her widowed mother at Seed House Farm, Samlesbury, and besides a servant girl, Mary Ann Wallace, they also employed a farmhand called John Joseph Atherton, aged seventeen. Atherton began to show affection towards Miss Worthington and his romantic advances were not welcomed. Consequently in late October he was dismissed from the farm, taking up employment at the nearby Roach Hall Farm.

On the third Sunday of December 1891 he turned up at Seed House Farm, Samlesbury armed with a revolver and lay in wait until he saw Miss Worthington and the servant girl make their way to the outhouse. He then knocked on the door and when Miss Worthington appeared he raised the revolver and fired at her. Struck with fear, she fell to the floor, dropping the lamp that she was carrying. Atherton quickly turned on his heels and fled the scene.

Assisted by Mary Ann, a shocked but apparently unharmed Miss Worthington returned to the farmhouse. She told her mother of the encounter and later that night she was to realise how fortunate she had been when the revolver was fired at her. As she undressed she heard a bullet fall on to the bedroom floor. It had penetrated all her clothing and was only stopped when it hit the steel stay of her corset.

Investigations on the following day showed that Atherton had paid a fleeting visit to Roach Hall Farm and had then been seen by another youth dashing through Preston Cemetery, after which the trail went cold.

Shortly after midnight on the Monday evening a youth walked into a police station in Chester and asked if he could warm himself by the fire. As he got into conversation with a police constable he told him that he had shot a young woman at Samlesbury, and he handed over some cartridges – the revolver was later found at Roach Hall farm. He was clearly under the impression that he had killed the girl, although communication with the police at Samlesbury showed that was not the case.

On the Wednesday he stood before the magistrates at Chester City police court charged with attempting to shoot Elizabeth Worthington. The next day he was handed over to PC Andrew Johnson from Samlesbury and a week later appeared before the magistrates at Bamber Bridge police court. After hearing evidence from Miss Worthington, described as a genteel-looking young lady, and from PC Johnson, who had found the revolver and a notebook full of ramblings about Atherton's affection for the young lady, the magistrates committed him for trial at the Lancaster Assizes of mid-March 1892 accused of attempted murder.

Mr McKeand defended Atherton by claiming he did not intend to murder Miss Worthington, and that he had become so passionate that he acted out of character.

His Lordship Mr Justice Coleridge described Atherton's actions as cowardly and unmanly. After consultation the jury delivered a verdict of attempting to commit grievous bodily harm, with a recommendation for mercy. His Lordship then told the prisoner that outrages of this kind could not be tolerated and passed a sentence of seven years' penal servitude.

Above left: A Victorian corset proved to be a lifesaver for Elizabeth Worthington.

Above middle: Mr McKeand spoke of the passion felt by the accused.

Above right: His Lordship Mr Justice Coleridge took a stern view of the crime.

Below: Atherton was last seen fleeing through Preston Cemetery.

EDWARDIAN BOYS ARE BIRCHED

On the third Wednesday of May 1904 two brothers, Morris Gilmor, aged thirteen, and Max Gilmor, aged ten, appeared in the dock at the Preston borough police court charged with stealing a purse containing 18 shillings belonging to Miss Alice Sloane of Fishwick Parade.

The prosecution case was presented by Mr Blackhurst, who told the magistrates that on the previous afternoon at around 4 o'clock Miss Sloane had been in Church Street when the lads followed her and pushed up against her. She had then entered a shop to purchase some oysters, with the elder lad following her there. After leaving the shop the lads again pushed up against her and when she got home she realised her purse was missing. She had immediately reported the theft to the police and the local constables were on the lookout for the lads.

PC Whitby was then called to testify and he told the court that while on patrol in Fishergate two boys approached him after seeing two lads pick a lady's pocket and run off with her purse. The constable, having been made aware of the theft, found her discarded and empty purse in a shop doorway. He had then observed the lads loitering near the railway station awaiting their mother's arrival from Blackpool and apprehended them.

When searched at the police station the elder lad was found to have a pocket full of coins including a couple of sovereigns, 4 florins and 7 shillings and a receipt for a £2 telegraph money order he had forwarded to his mother. When confronted with their crimes the brothers had confessed their guilt.

Their mother, a Jewish lady who was weeping bitterly, was then called into the witness box. In broken English she told the magistrates that she resided in Glasgow with her husband, where they kept a shop. Not feeling well, she had got a few pounds and taken the children to Blackpool, hoping the change would do her good. She, however, was running short of money and had intended to return home on the Tuesday. The lads were given their breakfast, and when she inquired for them later she was told they had not been seen. She had come on to Preston in the hope they would be there.

It was then stated that interviews with the lads had led to contradictory statements, although the elder lad had admitted to two or three robberies. The chairman of the magistrates., Dr Dunn, then addressed the mother and told her that no proper explanation of the boys conduct had been forthcoming from her and that the magistrates felt her explanation was feeble.

After retiring for a few minutes the magistrates returned to court and Dr Dunn addressed the lads. He informed the younger lad that he would be given six strokes with the birch, and the older lad, who ought to have known better, would, in addition to being fined 40 shillings, receive a dozen strokes of the birch. Upon hearing the sentences the mother and the lads burst into tears and there was some uproar in court before the lads were removed below.

Preston, Church Street.

Above: Edwardian Church Street where the juvenile pickpockets struck.

Right: Strokes of the birch were thought a fitting punishment in Edwardian days.

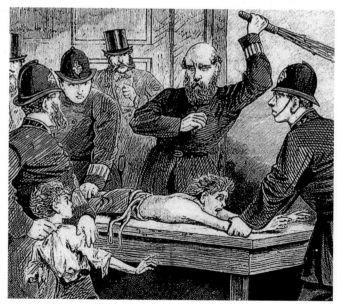

FROM RUSSIA WITHOUT LOVE

On the first Tuesday of April 1909 a dramatic tragedy unfolded within the Ashton area. That afternoon Miss Zena Tuzova, aged twenty-two, a young Russian lady, arrived at Preston railway station from Manchester with her companion Catherine McGregor. The two women went immediately to the General Post Office where Miss Tuzova sent a message by special courier to Harold Taylor, a gentleman whom she claimed she was engaged to, and who lived at the family home Lees Villa, Victoria Parade, in Ashton. She requested him to meet her that day in the Harris Free Library, but he did not show.

Consequently, that evening the ladies caught the tram to Ashton and turned up on his doorstep. The gentleman's brother, sister and mother all came to the door, but Harold refused to see her. With the door slammed, the young lady became hysterical

Miss Tuzova had waited for 'dear Harold' in the Harris Free Library.

WATERLOO ROAD, ASHTON-ON-RIBBLE, PRESTON.

The ladies caught the tram to the tranquil Waterloo Road and then walked to Victoria Parade, scene of the tragedy.

and appeared to swallow what was later discovered to be corrosive sublimate, a deadly mercury poison. She then flung herself against the vestibule door, crying out that she had taken poison and wanted to die. Eventually, a policeman calmed her down and the women went back to town by tram.

Later Miss Tuzova was seen on Friargate in a state of collapse and she was rushed to the Preston Royal Infirmary, where she died within hours. The coroner's inquest held at the hospital was told that in her bag was an engagement ring and a letter to 'Dear Harold' stating her intention to kill herself if rejected. Taylor had weeks earlier been with her in Manchester, but had returned home not wanting a relationship. The jury heard her last request was to be buried in a white dress with a violet ribbon, and they concluded that she had committed suicide while of unsound mind.

A SUFFRAGETTE'S MATTER FOR STARVATION

At the Liverpool Quarter Sessions in mid-July 1913 Mrs Edith Rigby, the wife of Dr Charles Rigby of Winckley Square, was accused of planting a bomb in the Exchange Buildings in Liverpool on 5 July. The court heard how a policeman on duty outside the building late that night heard a loud explosion and felt the ground beneath him shake.

Subsequent investigation led to the discovery of a gunpowder-packed cylinder, which had exploded in the basement. Fortunately, the device did not cause much damage and no one was injured. The search for the perpetrators had drawn a blank until four days after the explosion when Mrs Rigby presented herself at the Dale Street police station in Liverpool to admit to the offence, making a detailed confession of that crime and also taking responsibility for burning down the timber bungalow known as Roynton Cottage on Sir William Lever's Rivington estate in the same week.

Armed with paraffin, she had started a number of fires around the property and the bungalow had quickly caught fire, destroying the building along with valuable tapestries and works of art. These incidents were among a series of militant actions taken that summer by the national suffragette movement led by Mrs Pankhurst.

An active member of the group Mrs Rigby, aged forty, was taken into custody, but once in Walton Gaol she went on a hunger strike that led to her being released on bail prior to her trial. At her trial in late July there was no doubting her guilt, although she entered a plea to the contrary and was unwilling to name any accomplices, stating simply that she had been forced into her action by the government who had ignored the rights of women.

The Recorder of Liverpool, Edward Hemmerde, had little sympathy for her plight and she was sent to prison for nine months. Once again a hunger strike followed and within a fortnight she was in such a sick and feeble state that she was allowed to return home to recuperate. Once recovered she fled to Ireland for a brief spell and after returning home and leading a protest at the Public Hall in mid-October 1913 she was arrested again. Again Mrs Rigby chose to go on hunger strike and within days she was once more released from Walton Gaol to recuperate at home.

As things turned out, in August 1914, with Europe on the brink of war, Mrs Rigby penned a letter, published in the *Preston Herald*, stating that the Preston branch of the Women's Social and Political Union had suspended all militant action and were to concentrate on assisting the nation in the war efforts. With the suffragette movement taking a backseat, Mrs Rigby became an enthusiastic member of the new Land Army, digging for victory in the fields of Penwortham.

The former home of Edith Rigby on Winckley Square.

Inset: Edith Rigby, a great campaigner.

Eventually in 1918 those pioneering women such as Edith Rigby were rewarded for their loyalty by the introduction of the 'Women's Franchise Bill'. Then a decade later the victory was complete, when the women of the country aged over twenty-one received full enfranchisement by the introduction of the bill known at the time as 'The Flappers' Vote' by the Conservative government.

Edith Rigby was a valiant woman who endured calumny and derision so that women of the present day might have votes and social equality with men. In all, Edith Rigby lived a long and useful life and she enjoyed her existence to the full, despite being an invalid in her later years. She died in 1949 having served the cause of women's rights and been Preston's suffragette pioneer.

WIFE KILLING AT THE GRAPES HOTEL

In January 1914, John Jones, aged thirty-five, a former soldier with the Royal Field Artillery, married a woman of low repute called Mary. He was determined to reform his new wife and they set up home off Church Street in Preston. However, within six months his wife decided to resume her old ways and left her husband to live with another woman who was a prostitute.

Subsequently, when he saw his wife and her friend drinking in the Grapes Hotel (nowadays the Bears Paw) in mid-July 1914 he tried to persuade her to return home. She refused and an angry quarrel followed between the three of them. It ended with Jones grabbing his wife and running an open razor across her throat. Blood poured from her throat and she slumped to the floor. Jones next attempted to cut his own throat, but he was grabbed by shocked pub regulars. A constable was soon on the scene,

The Grapes Hotel (now the Bears Paw) on Church Street was the scene of tragedy in 1913.

A police illustrator sketched the drama that unfolded.

but Mary Jones, aged twenty-five, died within minutes and her killer was rushed to Preston Royal Infirmary with blood pouring from his wound.

Jones recovered from his injuries quickly and when questioned said simply: 'I married her off the streets and wanted to save her from further disgrace.' His trial in October 1914 at Lancaster Assizes led to a verdict of not guilty of murder, but guilty of manslaughter. His Lordship Justice Sankey took into account his previous good character and sentenced him to ten years' penal servitude.

There was much sympathy for Jones and his victim and thousands of people crowded into the Roman Catholic portion of the Preston Cemetery when her funeral took place. All the tramcars heading to the cemetery that day were full of mourners keen to pay their respects, many having fond memories of the Mary Ellis they knew before her short-lived marriage at St Joseph's months earlier.

POISON TRAGEDY OF JILTED SWEETHEART

In the year 1917 Marion Traynor, aged twenty-four, an Army Pay clerk was lodging in the home of Margaret Turner in Harland Street, Fulwood. On the first Wednesday of March Miss Traynor left her lodgings early, telling her landlady she would be back shortly.

By 8 o'clock that morning she was at the workshop of Joseph Noblett, a jeweller, whose premises were in Bamber's Yard. He and Miss Traynor had kept company for about 8 months, but had broken off their engagement in February, partly due to the fact that she was a Roman Catholic and he belonged to the Church of England. After the break up she had visited the workshop a number of times and talked about reconciliation. On this occasion she asked to talk with him, but he said he was busy and asked her to leave. She refused to go and so he went on with his work with his ex fiancée sat in the shop.

A couple of hours later when he came into the shop area she stood up and threw some pepper in his face, which prevented him from seeing for a little while. When he recovered his composure he noticed she had an empty bottle in her hand that had contained hydrochloric acid that she had taken from a shelf in the store. There was also an empty glass on the counter and she told him she had taken the poison. Within minutes she was doubled up in agony and Noblett quickly fetched her a glass of salt and water, and she began to vomit.

Alarmed at her condition Noblett rushed onto Friargate where he got the attention of PC Goodair who went back to the shop with him. The girl was still vomiting and was removed firstly to the police station on Lancaster Road where olive oil was administered, and then moved to the Preston Royal Infirmary. She had admitted taking the poison to PC Goodair, but told him she did not mean to do it.

Despite the best of medical attention she was in considerable pain and by early July she was moved to the Fulwood Workhouse Infirmary under the care of charge nurse Margaret Alice Wilson. Although by then she was able to take food well she was unable to retain it. Consequently her health deteriorated further and in mid-August 1917 she died.

An inquest was held at the Fulwood Workhouse on the third Friday of August before the coroner John Parker. Dr Pimley, medical officer of the Fulwood Workhouse, explained that the effects of the poison was that the girl became a skeleton. Cause of death being corrosion of the stomach due to the action of the acid.

Amongst those called was her ex fiancée Joseph Noblett who told the gathering she had struggled to come to terms with the ending of their relationship and stated that he was distraught over her drastic action. He explained that he had bottles of acid on the premises that he used for his business, but said he was not aware that she knew of their whereabouts.

Her landlady Margaret Turner described her as a young woman of an excitable disposition, but remarked that she had never heard her threaten to do anything to herself. She believed that she had no mother and had come from Liverpool to work.

The coroner concluded by saying there seemed no doubt that it was the girl's own act, being deeply disturbed by her engagement ending. In his opinion no blame could be attached to Noblett, who had acted in a proper manner. Evidence submitted suggested to him that she had gone to the shop in a very frenzied state, prepared to do something desperate.

After a lengthy consultation the jury returned a verdict of 'suicide whilst temporarily insane'.

Miss Traynor eventually died in the Fulwood Workhouse.

PICKPOCKETS MINGLE WITH THE PRESTON GUILD CROWDS

Unfortunately, the Preston Guild celebrations down the centuries, while attracting thousands of welcome visitors, did also attract a number of undesirables who mingled with the crowds. The Preston Guild held in September 1922 was notable for attracting over 600,000 visitors by train alone. Most were full of friendship, although a handful of undesirables were eager for thievery.

Straight after the Guild a special Preston Quarter Sessions dealt with a number of cases with police officers from other Lancashire forces attending as witnesses. Solomon Cohen, aged forty-five, from London and Joseph Freeman, aged fifty, from Leeds were charged with loitering with intent to steal. A detective had observed them among the crowds at the Agricultural Show on Moor Park, with Freeman seen putting his hand in the pocket of a man in front. The pair resisted arrest in a violent manner, but when charged admitted their guilt and were locked up for three months.

Pickpockets were lurking among the vast Preston Guild crowds of 1922.

From Victorian days the police were always trained to be extra vigilant.

Arthur Edwards, aged thirty-eight, of Birmingham and John Southall, aged forty-four, from London pleaded guilty to stealing a suitcase at the railway station. A detective had observed Southall picking up the suitcase and walking towards the exit with the co-accused. Both claimed it was a drunken prank, but were handed four-month sentences.

Norman Moore, aged twenty-eight, from Manchester and Ernest Mebson, aged twenty-four, of Sheffield were seen loitering on the fairground at Deepdale. A detective saw Moore lift the coats of three gentlemen and feel their hip pockets while Mebson and two others covered him. When one observed the detective they all scattered, but the two accused were caught. They had previous convictions for picking pockets and three months in prison was the verdict. Altogether nine cases of a similar nature were dealt with. While condemning the villains, chief magistrate Mr Firth expressed his pleasure that none of them were locals.

CRUCIAL FINGERPRINT
EVIDENCE OF ROBBERY

By the 1930s the admission of fingerprint evidence was beginning to play a crucial part in the detection of crime, but a trial at the Preston Sessions in May 1933 left the jury with a difficult decision to make.

Early in May labourer Robert Green, aged thirty-three, of Havelock Street, Preston, was brought before the Preston magistrates after being remanded in custody accused of breaking and entering the Stanleyfield Road Social Club a few days earlier. He pleaded not guilty, was granted legal aid and allowed bail until his trial in the middle of May.

The trial took place before Sir James Openshaw and the court heard that the door of the social club had been forced open and cigarettes, a bottle of whisky and £4 in cash had been taken. One of the witnesses was Detective Inspector Butler from Scotland Yard Fingerprints Bureau, who stated that prints had been found on a door jamb that corresponded to those of Robert Green. Inspector Butler passed enlarged photographs of the fingerprint from the crime scene and Green's corresponding fingerprint to the jury, telling them there were eighteen ridge characteristics that were in agreement and he was convinced they were as much a match as any in his sixteen years of fingerprint analysis.

Mr. R. Lambert, defending, pointed out a smear on one of the photographs and asked the witness if it was possible it could be hiding a discrepancy between the two exhibits. The witness replied by saying he could see under the smear quite clearly. To which response Mr Lambert countered by suggesting even he could be mistaken.

When Green was called he stated on oath that he knew nothing about the break in, did not even know where the club was, and that he had returned home at 7 o'clock that night after having a couple of drinks and went to bed at 11 o'clock, all evidence that was confirmed by his wife. Mr Lambert concluded his submissions by claiming the fingerprint evidence was not conclusive and that nothing else had been produced to link Green with the crime.

In summing up Sir James Openshaw told the jury that fingerprints were admissible evidence and it was up to their discretion if they accepted it or not. After retiring for a short time the jury returned a verdict of not guilty and the prisoner was discharged.

However, it was not the end of the matter as Green was arrested at the beginning of July accused of committing wilful perjury at his own trial at the Preston Sessions. The arrest followed an alleged conversation between Detective Constable Sumner and Green after a chance meeting at the Derby Arms in Lord Street in early June. According to the constable Green had said, 'I don't mind telling you now, as you can do nothing, as I was found not guilty. To tell the truth I only got five shillings out of it. They were my fingerprints all right. I agreed to keep my mouth shut as I had a

Above: A chance meeting in the Derby Arms on Lord Street led to a charge of perjury.

Below: Experts at work in the fingerprint department played a crucial role.

chance of getting out of it. When I was out on bail I went to the fellow who was on the job with me. I told him I would not pull him in. I had gone to bed with the missus and the fellow came afterwards to do the job. I will tell you what let you down. The fingerprint that was not developed, well, that was the other man.'

Green was arrested at his home the following day by Detective Sergeant Park and was remanded in custody charged with perjury. He appeared at the Preston borough police court two weeks later. When asked if he had anything to say he appeared distraught and remarked that the police were determined to shove him down, at which point his tearful wife was heard sobbing in the public gallery. He was then remanded overnight while a typed copy of the alleged conversation was made available to the magistrates.

The following day the police officers concerned gave their evidence and Green stated that while he was quite drunk when he had met Detective Constable Sumner he was sure he had not confessed his guilt. The other alleged burglar had been identified as James Brown, who was serving three months in Liverpool prison. He was called and stated that the pair had not committed the crime. The chairman Mr. W. H. Francis then retired with the other magistrates to consider the submissions. When he returned he informed Green he would be discharged as they thought there was not sufficient evidence for the case to go before a jury.

FULWOOD BARRACKS HAUNTING TALES AND A FORGOTTEN KILLER

If you delve into the past of Fulwood Barracks, there are a number of harrowing events that took place there since its opening in 1848 and consequently there have been tales of ghosts and ghouls. Back in 1861 the murder of Colonel Crofton and Captain Hanham by the young Private Patrick McCaffrey was a shocking affair. With a single rifle shot he killed both officers and within weeks was hanged outside Kirkdale Gaol by executioner William Calcraft. In later years it was claimed that the ghost of Patrick McCaffrey haunted the officers' mess.

In February 1903 Bombardier Harry Short was found dead in his bed with a bullet wound through his head. He had been slain by Gunner William George Hudson, whose subsequent trial recorded a guilty verdict. Within days he was hanged by executioner William Billington within Strangeways Prison, Manchester. Not surprisingly this event led to more tales of ghostly sightings within the barracks' dormitories.

Even the garrison chapel of St Alban is said to be haunted by some mysterious spirit. An apparition near to the pulpit is the common claim, with objects said to have moved mysteriously. Then there is the reported sighting of a battalion of Roman soldiers marching across the parade ground along the line of the original Watling Street Road of Roman construction. There are also well-documented accounts of the early twentieth-century spirit of the old officers' mess. Apparently this phantom figure has scared a soldier or two in its own haunting way.

Certainly, those events have contributed to the spine-chilling image of Fulwood Barracks around Halloween. However, one melancholy incident from the more recent past is every bit as frightful as those events of old.

The events of a July day in 1939 would lead to a soldier stationed at Fulwood Barracks having a date with the hangman on the morning of Halloween of that year. A Halloween execution awaited Sergeant Raymond Smith, aged thirty-four, a member of the 2nd Battalion of the Loyal Regiment.

On the second Sunday of July 1939 Sgt Smith, along with his wife, who was pregnant, attended a gathering in the sergeants' mess, spending the evening in the company of his friend Sgt Wilkinson and his wife. The couples had a pleasant time and headed back to their quarters in West Block shortly after eleven o'clock.

Two hours later Sgt Smith walked into the guardroom partly dressed and asked for the telephone number of the Fulwood police station. Having got through to the police, his comments stunned the guards in the room as he declared, 'I have murdered my wife and daughter. Send the police at once.'

The police were there within minutes and a harrowing scene awaited in Sgt Smith's quarters, with his wife, Elizabeth, aged thirty-five, and their daughter Joan, aged four, laying in their beds with bullet wounds in their heads. Mrs Smith was dead and her daughter, although still breathing, was to die two hours later in the hospital.

When taken into custody Smith readily admitted the shootings and claimed he had tried to end his own life in the same way but could not reach the rifle trigger, showing the police a live cartridge and saying it was meant for himself. In the family quarters the police had found his army rifle and the spent cartridges used for the killings.

Smith had been adamant that he was not insane and that he had killed his family because he could not face life without them. Due in Aldershot in a week's time, prior to being posted abroad, he said he could not stand the thought of leaving his wife, who was four months pregnant, behind.

When he appeared at the Preston county police court charged with the double killing, details of the terrible tragedy left a feeling of puzzlement among those gathered. Sgt Smith, from Stoke originally, had been regarded as a devoted husband and father who had been in the army since 1924 and had been at Fulwood Barracks since 1932 with a number of spells abroad.

A statement from Smith included the following: 'I decided to commit suicide and take my family with me. I walked into the bedroom and shot my wife and then my daughter. I then tried to commit suicide by placing the muzzle of the rifle to my head and pulling the trigger. I could not reach the trigger and gave up after several attempts. Then I attempted to gas myself, switching the gas full on and putting my head in the oven without success. I then walked to the guardhouse and telephoned the police.'

His mental health had been regarded pivotal to his actions and in his defence it was claimed that there was no murder motive nor was it a case of either party being unfaithful. As the proceedings closed Smith was committed for trial at the forthcoming Lancaster Assizes in early October. In the weeks that followed Smith was under observation at Walton Gaol and latterly at Durham Prison with regard to his mental state.

Sensational as Sgt Smith's actions had been, they paled into the background at Fulwood Barracks when news arrived of the beginning of the Second World War in early September. When his trial got underway only a handful of people occupied the public gallery to listen to Mr. Justice Cassells opening remarks. Details of the tragedy were repeated and there was no doubt that Smith was the killer. However, the defence lawyer claimed that he had allowed anxiety to prey on his mind, and when his brain snapped he destroyed those most precious to him. In his summing up His Lordship said although the jury had been invited to bring in a verdict of guilty but insane, this might not be the case. The jury took just half an hour to return a guilty verdict, dismissing any insanity claims. Mr Justice Cassells then placed the black cap on his head and, looking at the accused, sentenced him to death in the usual manner. As Smith was being taken down he turned to a couple of army colleagues and mouthed a goodbye.

Within days it was announced that Sgt Smith would be executed at Walton Gaol on the day of Halloween in 1939, with chief hangman Thomas Pierrepoint the intended executioner. Smith was a man in torment who appeared somewhat relieved that he would soon be delivered into eternity. He was in contact with his lawyers in Preston, expressing a desire not to appeal against the verdict, nor against his execution.

Despite this request Mr Henry Fazackerley, who had organised Sgt Smith's defence and called it a crime of affection, went ahead with an appeal as Smith waited in the condemned cell. With just seventy-two hours to go he was told that the Home Secretary Sir John Anderson had seen fit to reprieve him. Destined to spend a life imprisoned during His Majesty's Pleasure the former soldier's torment would continue.

When Halloween came around in 1939 the soldiers of Fulwood Barracks had more pressing matters, with the call to arms and many a battle to be fought. As the war exploits of the Fulwood Barracks-based soldiers took the headlines Sgt Smith became the forgotten killer and down the decades it is Patrick McCaffrey, Gunner Hudson and even Jessica Black, the jewel thief who stole a diamond ring, the property of Mrs Crofton, the widow of the unfortunate Colonel Crofton, who have had their crimes more often recalled.

It is, of course, true to say that the military men of Fulwood Barracks have certainly served a useful purpose in the town in times gone by. For instance, during the cotton famine of 1863, when the famished workers rioted, it was a body of 250 infantry soldiers with fixed bayonets who managed to quell the troubles. Battalions have come and gone and Preston has had cause to delight at its military men who have served their country far and wide.

What truth lays within the tales of ghostly goings leaves us all to wonder, but the reality is that Fulwood Barracks is very much part of Preston's colourful history. Like me though, just in case, perhaps best to stay well away on Halloween.

Right: Fulwood Barracks has had its share of tragic and haunting times.

Below: There was tragedy within the Fulwood Barracks married quarters in 1939.

Inset: Mr Justice Cassells sentenced the soldier to death.

A BRIEF ENCOUNTER ON PRESTON RAILWAY STATION

Throughout the years of the Second World War the buffet bar at Preston railway station was a welcome place for those in the armed forces, with hundreds of volunteers serving countless cups of tea for free to refresh the weary travellers. On Boxing Day evening 1941 serving soldier Simon Lamb, aged twenty-six, a Preston man on a three-day leave, had been to Lancaster for the day and popped into the tearoom prior to going home. An ATS girl caught his eye and after a brief conversation he learnt she was off to London. He told her he was off to the same place and they made their way on to the platform to await the train. When the train arrived he told her he was going to get his suitcase, entering the carriage with one he had randomly taken off a luggage trolley.

As the train sped through Warrington he confessed to the girl that he had stolen it, and after forcing it open he found it contained three suits, two pairs of shoes

Lamb helped himself to unattended luggage at Preston railway station.

Inset: An ATS poster girl – the girls were always popular with the troops.

and some women's clothing. The girl told him he would have no trouble selling it on. Shortly after midnight, as most of the passengers snoozed the night away, he quietly snatched a handbag from besides a sleeping lady, helped himself to £5 and then returned it.

When they reached London early on a chilly morning the couple stayed at the YMCA for a few hours. Then they took a taxi to the West End where the girl knew a man who would buy the suitcase and its contents. The transaction complete and with an extra £3 to spend, the pair spent the day visiting numerous public houses. That night they cuddled up in an air-raid shelter in central London. By dawn it was time to say goodbye, with Simon Lamb hitchhiking back to Preston.

Almost a fortnight later he turned up at Preston police station, telling the desk sergeant he was an absentee from the army and wished to give himself up. He then volunteered the information about the stolen suitcase and confessed to having taken some postal packets at Carlisle. The next day he was up before the Preston magistrates and details of his confession to Detective Falconer were read out. He pleaded guilty to the thefts and as a result of his brief encounter, he was sent to prison for six months.

MYSTERY OF THE MISSING SILK STOCKINGS

During the Second World War to own a pair of fully fashioned silk stockings was quite a luxury for any lady. The scarcity of them in the days of food and clothing ration books add to their value. This was highlighted in mid-June 1942 when two women and three men appeared before a special sitting of the Preston borough magistrates, charged with conspiring to steal parcels and goods in transit on the London, Midland & Scottish Railway.

It was alleged that they were substituting labels on parcels and cartons, which resulted in silk stockings and shirts, valued at over £160, being delivered to wrong addresses in Preston. The magistrates heard that besides the conspiracy charge the two women, Violet Ellen Parr, twenty-eight, and Susannah Slater, fifty-one, were both accused of receiving. While Jeremiah Collins, fifty-two, employed as a checker by the LMS Railway, was charged with five thefts, George Lang, forty-eight, an aircraft worker, was charged with three counts of receiving and Arthur Parr, thirty-five, a temporary railway porter, was accused of being an accessory to theft.

Parcels that in January, February and March should have gone to leading Preston retailers British Home Stores, Middlebrooks, Lingards and Bleazards were instead redirected. Among the witnesses was Thomas Coupe, who stated that he had been visited by George Lang at his draper's shop in Orchard Street in January, saying he could put some goods his way if he was interested. He had declined the offer, but agreed to receive some parcels for him, which arrived in the following weeks and which Lang collected. Eventually, Coupe grew suspicious of the parcels and refused to receive any more.

Another witness testified as to having visited Lang's home in Lea and having purchased stockings and shirts from him. A couple of LMS Railway carters then testified to delivering parcels to Percy Street where Susannah Slater signed for them, and witnesses stated that Violet Ellen Parr had sold them silk stockings, claiming they were from Marks & Spencer. A search of the home of Mr and Mrs Parr unearthed some of the missing items and wrappings from the parcels delivered there. The combined investigations of the Preston borough police, Lancashire Constabulary and LMS Railway police had delivered enough evidence for the magistrates to send all five accused for trial at the next Preston Sessions in mid-July 1942.

The Preston Sessions were held before His Honour Judge Fraser Harrison, and Susannah Slater and her daughter Violet Ellen Parr pleaded guilty to charges of receiving and Jeremiah Collins pleaded guilty to five charges of theft and one of conspiracy. During the trial George Lang's defence was that Collins had relabelled

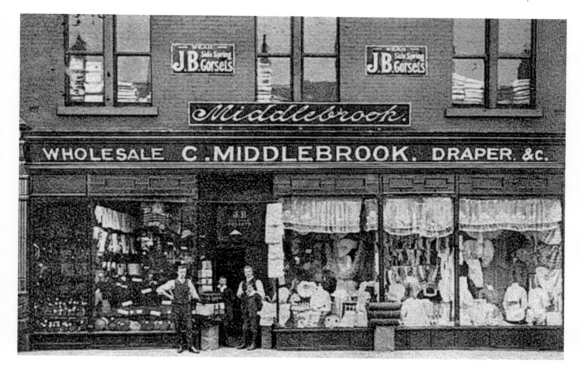

Above: Local store Middlebrooks did not receive their supply of silk stockings.

Right: The 1940s alternative to silk stockings.

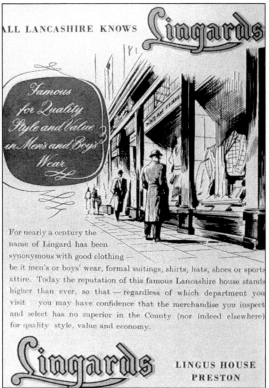
Above left: Silk stockings were a luxury wartime item.

Above right: Shirts for Lingard's Preston store went missing.

parcels to him against his wishes and it became apparent that the only evidence against Arthur Parr was accusations from Collins. After lengthy submissions during which it was suggested the women had been under the influence of others the jury retired.

They returned with guilty verdicts against Lang and he was sent to prison for fifteen months; Arthur Parr was found not guilty and discharged; the two women, who seemed to have the sympathy of Judge Fraser Harrison, were found not guilty of conspiracy and were bound over for two years for receiving. Having pleading guilty earlier, Jeremiah Collins was then informed he would be imprisoned for nine months with hard labour.

A FLEEING FUGITIVE SHOOTS AT POLICE

On the second Saturday of March 1947 there was drama on Preston's streets when a gun-wielding thief was pursued by the police. The incident began when a car was stolen in Blackpool and abandoned in Starch House Square, with the driver, seen by PC Thorley, dashing off into Friargate and then to Bamber's Yard. The officer and another man gave pursuit, only to be stopped in their tracks when the fugitive produced a pistol and fired towards the constable, the bullet piercing his topcoat.

The man then got on a bus wielding the pistol and threatened the driver, before eventually jumping off in Corporation Street and disappearing. It emerged that the man was James Heaton, twenty-five, a bricklayer from Preston who had been on the run from early February after a bungled armed robbery at a boarding house on Fishergate Hill.

He was eventually arrested at Kings Cross station in London in late March and brought back to Preston to be sent for trial at Liverpool Assizes. An attempted murder charge was dropped, but robbery with violence, breaking and entering and attempting to cause grievous bodily harm by shooting were among the charges he faced.

He claimed he only used the pistol to scare his pursuers off, but the jury had no hesitation in finding him guilty. His Lordship Mr Justice MacNaghten described him as a very dangerous criminal, commenting on the prisoner's long criminal history from his youth, before handing him a fourteen-year prison sentence.

The fuguitive ran down Bamber's Yard and along St George's Road.

A SHOCKING CASE OF INSANITY AT WHITTINGHAM

Opened ironically on April Fools' Day 1873, the Whittingham Asylum served the community of Lancashire and during its heyday in the mid-1930s it was home to over 3,000 patients. The hospital expanded down the decades and it was more or less self-sufficient with officers' residences, cottages for gardeners, stables, farm buildings, workshops, blacksmiths, laundry, post office, reservoirs and its own railway from Grimsargh. Despite the picture of an idyllic village life there were a number of tragic and traumatic events that took place.

Among the inmates from 1928 was Albert Pickles, a former weaver from Burnley, who had been admitted aged twenty-seven. His stay at Whittingham was to end in dramatic fashion on the last Wednesday of September 1951. The events of that afternoon were recalled the following Wednesday when Jack Hooley, aged thirty-three, another patient at Whittingham, appeared before the Preston county magistrates accused of the murder of Albert Pickles.

The court heard that at around 4 o'clock Fred Stanton, a charge nurse, made an inspection of Ward 19 in the old annex. He saw Pickles busily dusting in the second-floor dormitory, accompanied by another patient. While downstairs on the first floor was the accused and several other patients carrying out domestic duties.

Shortly after Stanton had returned to the ground floor, the patient who had been with Pickles rushed down the stairs and informed him that Pickles had been attacked. Rushing upstairs he found Pickles on the floor in a pool of blood between two beds. He was obviously in a critical state and by the time the female doctor arrived he was dead. A later post-mortem examination showed that he had died from fourteen stab wounds in his chest, back and head that caused haemorrhaging.

Hooley's coat and shirt were covered with blood after the incident and eventually a homemade dagger – a piece of sharpened steel with a bound handle – was found hidden in a storage room. According to Stanton when he confronted the accused he had said, 'I did it. I'd rather tell the police'.

According to the prosecution the accused was the lone aggressor, being the only patient with blood on their clothing and was someone who took the opportunity to do this terrible thing without thinking of the consequences.

After hearing all the evidence Chairman Sir William Ascroft looked towards Hooley and asked him if he had anything to say before the court ordered his committal for trial at the next Liverpool Assizes. Acting against the advice of his solicitor, Hooley, who was a native of Blackpool, read out a statement from the dock, telling the court: 'The reason why I killed Albert Pickles was because of the conflict from evil forces trying to make me deny the holy God'. Hooley was then ordered to be detained in Walton Gaol until his trial a couple of weeks later.

During his time in Walton Gaol he was examined by Dr Quinn, a medical officer at the prison, who addressed the court at the Liverpool Assizes, stating that Hooley was suffering from paranoia or persecution mania. His Lordship Mr Justice Stables, after hearing the facts and consulting with the solicitors, came to his conclusions, informing the accused that he was deemed unfit to plead due to insanity and that he would be detained at the king's pleasure. Hooley faced a life under padlock and key rather than the relative freedom of Whittingham.

With the advance of medical treatments by the 1960s for mentally sick patients the Victorian asylums were beginning to lose favour and the inevitable closure of Whittingham arrived in 1995.

Above: It was a village-like setting at Whittingham.

Below: The killing took place within an annex building of Whittingham.

DEATH SENTENCE FOR ST GEORGE'S ROAD KILLER

On the second Monday of October 1956 Frank Smart, aged thirty-nine, a cook of Jamaican origin who lived in Berkley Street, Liverpool, caught the bus to Preston. His intended destination was St George's Road where his estranged wife, Catherine, aged thirty-seven, also a West Indian, was cohabiting with fellow countryman Fitz Evan Rattan, aged forty, in lodgings above a shop at the corner of Kent Street.

What followed in mid-afternoon was a tragedy that stunned local residents. An emergency telephone call led to the swift appearance of police officers at the address where in the scullery they discovered the lifeless body of Rattan with a stab wound to the chest. Catherine Smart, who had staggered into a local shop with visible wounds to her throat and face, was rushed off to hospital where she died shortly afterwards. The police, led by Chief Constable Frank Richardson, acted swiftly and Smart was apprehended near to the crime scene, telling the police, 'I am the man you want'. The following morning Smart appeared before the Preston magistrates, being charged initially with the murder of Rattan and remanded in custody.

In mid-February 1957 the accused stood trial at Liverpool Assizes and only the charge of murdering his wife was brought before the jury. The court heard that on the fateful afternoon Herman Boddoe, a fellow West Indian, had gone upstairs with Rattan and Mrs Smart to their bedsit room. Shortly afterwards the door opened and Smart rushed in. He put a small case at the foot of the bed and took out what Beddoe described as a long parcel. He hurriedly tore it open and produced a ferocious-looking knife. According to Beddoe the accused then said to his wife: 'You think that you can hide from me, but wherever you go I can track you down like a bloodhound.'

Beddoe then questioned Smart's right to behave so aggressively to his wife and he responded by saying: 'I have come for her. The only way I will not get her is if I am dead.' After some heated discussions Smart leapt at Rattan and stabbed him in the chest. He then began waving the weapon in front of his wife and inflicted a number of wounds before fleeing the scene.

In his defence Smart claimed that Ratten had been aggressive towards him and that his wife had lunged at him with a lemonade bottle. However, examination of the bottle had shown no sign of Mrs Smart's fingerprints upon it.

When the prosecutor, Mr Nahum, addressed the jury he stated that if Smart brandished the knife at his wife with intent to kill or do serious harm to her, then it was simply a case of murder, undoubtedly an act of jealousy and revenge.

Mr Robertson Crighton, defending, pleaded that Smart, who had been discharged from the Trinidad Army for instability, did not intend to kill his wife. He also revealed that when Smart had found out about his wife's indiscretions with Rattan he had taken a mixture of rat poison and iodine in an attempt to take his own life.

Murder scene at the junction of St George's Road and Kent Street.

Inset: Mr Justice Streatfield passed a sentence of death.

Mr Justice Streatfield warned the jury not to let their good judgement be clouded by sympathy for a wronged husband. After less than two hours the jury returned with a guilty verdict. His Lordship then proceeded to pass the sentence of death in the usual manner. The tall and bespectacled Smart was then removed from the dock to await execution.

Smart's solicitors immediately began proceedings to appeal against the sentence. Within weeks Smart was reprieved and given a life sentence for the tragic crime. He was clearly distraught at the thought of life in prison and in late May 1957 he threw himself over the landing railings of his third-floor cell at Walton Gaol, landing on the wire mesh safety net below. Rushed to hospital in an unconscious state and bleeding from a head wound, he died within hours. An inquest followed and a verdict of suicide was recorded.

LANDLADY SLAUGHTERED AT THE KENDAL CASTLE

On the last Saturday of May 1962 the landlord of the Kendal Castle public house, on the corner of Ladyman Street in Preston, went for a day out with some regulars to Thirsk racecourse. That evening, when the barmaid Pauline Green arrived for work at six o'clock, she found the landlady, Mary Salter, aged fifty-eight, lying dead on the kitchen floor in a pool of blood. Some cigarettes had been stolen and money taken from the till behind the bar.

Inquiries led to a pub regular named Bernard Joseph McCrorey, aged twenty-nine, who lived in Latham Street and had been spending money freely. It transpired that he had hidden in the toilets at closing time that afternoon and attacked Mrs Salter with a hammer when she caught him rifling through the till.

At the Manchester Assizes trial of McCrorey in July 1962 it was claimed in his defence that the killing had not been premeditated and that it should be

The Kendal Castle in May 1962.

Barmaid Pauline Green made a horrific discovery.

manslaughter, not murder. Alex Karmel QC, appearing for the prosecution, described it as a brutal and horrifying murder with at least eight hammer blows having been inflicted on the head of the defenceless woman. When questioned by the police McCrorey admitted to the crime, saying it was a nightmare and had occurred on the spur of the moment when the landlady had spotted him.

The jury took over four hours before returning a verdict of capital murder and McCrorey was sentenced to hang. The Preston lass to whom he had been married for less than a year and his mother who had come from Canada to witness the trial both wept as the killer was sent down.

A provisional date was set for his execution, but an appeal was launched by his solicitor Derek Fazackerley, who once again claimed the killing was not premeditated. In late July 1962 Lord Chief Justice Parker ruled that a verdict of manslaughter was to be substituted, along with a life sentence for the Kendal Castle killer.

Derek Fazackerley was a partner in the Preston firm of Smith, Fazackerley & Co. He became a deputy coroner in 1961, progressing to county coroner in 1967. He gained a reputation for being a controversial coroner who was often critical of councils and government. It was something of a surprise in June 1972 when he decided to quit his county coroner role and retire at the age of fifty-two. Preston folk were shocked to hear the news in February 1979 that Derek Fazackerley had died less than seven years after his early retirement.

As for the Kendal Castle it was known in later years as simply the Castle before it closed its doors for the last time in 2007 and was converted into residential apartments.

CAPITAL PUNISHMENT FOR PRESTON PAIR

In the summer of 1964 the debate over the abolition of hanging was at its height and Preston was to find itself in the national spotlight as two of the town's residents faced execution.

The drama had begun to unfold early in April when John Alan West, a fifty-three-years old van driver for the Lakeland Laundry, was found dead in his Workington home. The discovery of his body, which had been bludgeoned and stabbed in the heart in the early hours of the morning, led to a murder hunt. A search of the house revealed a raincoat that did not belong to the victim and in one of the pockets was a medallion inscribed with the following: 'G.O. Evans July 1961'.

The police took little time to trace Gwynne Owen Evans, the owner of the raincoat, to his lodgings in Clarendon Street, Preston. A search of the house led to the discovery of a length of steel-lined tubing thought to be one of the murder weapons and to the discovery of a gold wrist watch engraved with the name of John Alan West in the lining of the jacket of his friend, Peter Anthony Allen.

Both men were immediately arrested and under interrogation blamed each other for the killing. Evans, who had once worked with the victim, claimed that Allen had repeatedly hit their victim about the head. There were signs of a terrific struggle with blood marks suggesting a number of blows being struck from the top to the bottom of the stairs where West was found. Allen stated that Evans had claimed it would be an easy touch and that no violence would be necessary.

The pair had gone to West's home that night to try to borrow money from him and Allen's wife and children had also gone along for the ride. Mary Allen and her children had remained in the vehicle, which had been stolen two days earlier, while the two men visited West's home. The car was spotted at Windermere on the way back and it was there that a police dog discovered the red-handled knife used in the killing.

The two Preston dairymen stood trial at the beginning of July 1964 at Manchester Crown Court and it lasted seven days. Allen insisted that Evans had done the stabbing and both continued to insist that the other was the killer. When the jury retired to consider the evidence they took just over three hours to return a guilty verdict against both men. Mr Justice Ashworth then passed a sentence of death on both for the capital murder of the Cumberland man.

With feelings strongly in favour of the abolition of the death penalty, the two condemned men soon had vigorous campaigns going for their reprieve. The Lord Chief Justice, who remarked, 'A more brutal murder would be difficult to imagine', dismissed an early appeal against their sentence.

Nevertheless, the campaign continued in the three weeks that remained before the date of execution. The curate of Preston parish church led calls for mercy from his pulpit and he was out on the streets with other campaigners gathering signatures for a petition to the Home Secretary. Over a thousand names were on the document delivered to the Home Secretary but he found no reason to intervene. Family and friends then made a plea for clemency to the Queen but this was unsuccessful as well.

On Thursday 13 August 1964 the two men were executed at 8 o'clock in the morning. Peter Anthony Allen, aged twenty-one, was hanged at Walton Prison, Liverpool, and at the same time Gwynne Owen Evans, aged twenty-four, was hanged at Strangeways Prison, Manchester. A silent demonstration took place in their adopted town of Preston and protestors held vigils outside both prisons as the executions took place.

As things transpired the two killers were making history, as they were the last to suffer a sentence of death after the bill suspending capital punishment in Great Britain was brought into force in November 1965. Their punishment earned them a place to this day in the Guinness Book Of Records for being the last to feel the hangman's noose around their necks.

Robert Leslie Stewart, who was born in Edinburgh and lived in Oldham, hanged Allen, while Evans met his fate at the hands of the other official executioner, Harry Allen, a Manchester man who, like his colleague, had been an assistant to Albert Pierrepoint, a well-known local executioner. With redundancy looming, Allen and Stewart could reflect on a seven-year spell in which they had carried out thirty-four executions.

The Preston dairymen were the last in a long line of local folk who had a date with the hangman. In the nineteenth and early twentieth century a number of local cases attracted much public interest. Back in 1827 young mother Jane Scott was hanged at Lancaster Castle for the poisoning of her parents after feeding them porridge laced with arsenic. In 1861 private soldier Patrick McCaffery was hanged outside Kirkdale Gaol, Liverpool, for the killing of two army officers at Fulwood Barracks. Four years later Preston tailor Stephen Burke was hanged outside Lancaster Castle for the murder of his wife at their desolate cottage home in Brunswick Street, William Calcraft, the official executioner, performing the task. Ten years later another Preston wife killer, Mark Fiddler, suffered the same fate, although this time the execution was carried out inside the castle after the ending of public executions.

Several hundred folk gathered outside Strangeways Prison in Manchester in November 1881 to see the black flag hoisted after the execution of John Aspinall Simpson, who had slain his sweetheart, Annie Ratcliffe, the daughter of the landlord of the Blue Bell Inn on Church Street.

Another killing of a sweetheart six years later led to the hanging of pawnbrokers assistant Alfred Sowrey after his conviction for the murder of Annie Kelly, a maid from the Bull Head Hotel.

Stonemason Thomas Riley was arrested in 1883 for the murder of local woman Elizabeth Alston in Back Dock Street after a drunken liaison. His plight gathered much local sympathy but despite a petition with 7,000 signatures he was also hanged at Strangeways.

Preston widow Isabella Cookson was sentenced to hang in April 1898 after being found guilty of causing the death of her newly born grandchild. The tearful woman had her sentenced commuted to one of penal servitude for life after pleas on her behalf.

Fulwood Barracks was the scene of another brutal murder in 1903 when Bombardier Short was found shot in the head. His convicted killer, Gunner William George Hudson, was executed on a May morning at Strangeways Prison.

In April 1906 butcher's wife Alice Dewhurst escaped the hangman by being declared insane following her fatal knife-wielding attack on her husband at their Church Street shop. Within months she had committed suicide at the Broadmoor Asylum.

Also in that year the town was gripped by the killing of James Fell at his warehouse in St John's Place and the trials that followed. Two men stood accused, with Paddy Callaghan eventually convicted and sentenced to death. Believing he was innocent, local campaigners worked tirelessly to save him from the hangman and his sentence was commuted to penal servitude for life. After twenty long years he was freed and returned to Preston still claiming that he had been wrongly convicted.

Above left: Peter Anthony Allen (top) and Gwynne Owen Evans (bottom), who became the last pair to hang in Great Britain.

Above right: The Dewhurst family in happier times.

Left: Clarendon Street in Preston where the killers had lodgings.

HUNT FOR KILLERS OF THE MAN IN WHITE

A brutal killing in Preston in 1971 provided a glimpse into the twilight world unfamiliar to everyday folk.

William Zezzerz was considered a little eccentric and was described as a loner who often wandered the streets of Preston wearing a white jacket, trousers and a white baseball cap that earned him the nickname the 'man in white'. Shortly before midnight on the last Thursday of July 1971 he was seen walking past the Rosebud Inn on the corner of London Road flanked by a man and a woman. Early the following morning the police were informed that some children had found the body of a man in a lobby between two derelict houses close to where William Zezzerz had been seen the night before. After some painstaking investigation the police learnt that the person who had met a violent death was sixty-year-old William Zezzerz, who lodged in a bedsit in Christian Road.

In early December 1971 Patrick Joseph Campbell, aged thirty-nine, and Barbara Flood, aged thirty-two, both of no fixed address, appeared at the Liverpool Crown Court accused of murder and entered pleas of not guilty. According to the prosecution, led by David Waddington QC, the pair had been seen in the company of Mr Zezzerz on London Road on the night before the battered body had been found. He had been attacked in a ferocious and brutal manner and four bloodstained bricks had been found nearby.

A local prostitute was among those who gave evidence and she testified that she had been in a derelict house behind the Rosebud Inn with a client when she heard the sound of shouting, scuffling and banging. She claimed that she heard Flood say the victim had insulted her and the deathly commotion had followed. When all went quiet her client quickly departed and she followed him a few moments later, tripping over the body of Mr Zezzerz in the alleyway as she fled. The following night she saw Campbell in the Red Lion public house on Church Street and told him she knew what he had done to the old fellow, advising him to get out of town. Campbell responded by saying he had been drunk and could not remember what he had done.

The court heard that Campbell had been questioned by police at his lodgings in West Park Avenue, Ashton, early on the Friday morning after they had received a report of him collapsing in the street in a drunken state. Eventually admittance to his lodgings was gained and although he had blood on his clothing there was no reason to connect him with the appalling crime at that time.

The prosecution stated that when Barbara Flood had been questioned she had become distressed, telling the police that it started out as a rolling job and she didn't realise Campbell would kill him. Having seen Zezzera on London Road Campbell had said to her, 'I will see if I can get some money off him'. She claimed that Campbell had pushed the victim down the lobby and after hearing some blows Campbell had returned and handed her a £5 note.

The jury, after a retirement of three hours, returned to announce a verdict of not guilty of murder but guilty of manslaughter. Mr Justice Bean then addressed the culprits, saying they had been convicted of a truly terrible killing of a man who had never done either of them any harm. He went on to say that while it was Campbell who had done the actual killing she had been a party to the horrendous crime. Campbell was then handed a prison sentence of eight years and Flood was sent to gaol for four years.

Above: William Zezzerz had been seen walking past the Rosebud Inn shortly before he was brutally killed.

Left: A local prostitute, aware of the killing, confronted Campbell in the Red Lion on Church Street the next day.

REVENGE KILLING OF JUDGE OPENSHAW

Judge William Harrison Openshaw was born in Southport and educated at Harrow and Cambridge. He was the chairman of the County Quarter Sessions from 1958 until the courts were reorganised in the early 1970s. Judge Openshaw then became a judge on the northern circuit and was given the honorary title of recorder of Preston. In that role he became a familiar figure at the town's numerous civic ceremonies. Highly distinguished in his judicial robes and standing 6 feet 6 inches tall, he often stood head and shoulders above the rest. Married with two sons and a daughter, he earned the love and respect of all who worked closely with him. A genial giant to his friends and staff, he was a lawyer who dealt firmly in his judgement of the people of violence.

Therefore, Preston was stunned on the second Tuesday of May 1981 when the sixty-eight-year-old judge was stabbed to death at his Park House home on Garstang Road in Broughton. After grappling with an intruder he was found bleeding badly on the driveway of his home by his wife Joyce. A murder investigation was swiftly underway to capture a man who, heavily bloodstained, had been seen running from the house shortly after 8 o'clock in the morning. The attacker had leapt over a fence at the rear of the property and made off across fields. He had then flagged down a motorist, brandished the sheath knife used to kill the judge and ordered the driver to head to the motorway. Scotland was his intended destination and eventually he bound and gagged the motorist and dumped him on a remote country lane.

The police were quickly on the killer's tail and in the Border region of Scotland, after a police chase, he was apprehended and taken to Hawick police station where, after a brief appearance before the local sheriff, he was handed over to Lancashire detectives.

John Smith appeared in court accused of murder.

Left: Forensic experts were soon at the Park House murder scene.

Below: The gateway to murder these days, with a housing development emerging on the site of Park House at Broughton.

Inset: Judge William Harrison Openshaw, victim of a revenge killer.

The man remanded in custody was called John Smith, aged thirty-one, who had been living in Burnley. At his trial at Leeds Crown Court it was revealed that Smith had borne a long-standing grievance against the British penal system ever since being sent to Borstal by Judge Openshaw in 1968. As recently as 1980 he had spent a lengthy period sitting at the top of Blackpool Tower as a protest against the system. Branded a danger to society, he was given a life sentence for the murder with a recommendation that he serve at least twenty-five years for the cold-blooded murder.

PENRITH HOUSE KILLER BROUGHT TO JUSTICE

On the second Thursday of December 1982, during the late afternoon, Bernard Billington and his girlfriend Carole Burke walked into the Penrith House flat of their friend Mary McLeish and saw a horrific sight. They discovered their friend Mary half naked and bleeding heavily from head wounds, with Indian neighbour Kanti Patel lying on top of her. The pair claimed they entered the lounge just as Patel was attempting to have sex with the lifeless woman. After being discovered Patel attempted to leave the flat but was forcibly stopped by Billington, who detained him until the police arrived.

At the trial of Kanti Patel in September 1983 at Manchester Crown Court he denied killing the mother of seven. The court was told that the unemployed Patel often used the affectionate term 'mother' with regards to Mary McLeish, who, aged fifty-two, was seven years older than him. A witness testified that a few hours before the incident

The Avenham Park Inn, where the pair had been drinking together earlier that day.

Shortly after Patel left the Jalgo's club on Rose Street his victim Mary McLeish was found dead.

the pair had been drinking together in the nearby Avenham Park Inn. Statements also placed Patel at the nearby Jalgo's club in mid-afternoon and neighbours were called who claimed they had heard raised voices, although not necessarily with an Asian accent, in the apartment shortly after Patel left the Jalgo's club.

Forensic evidence was submitted that indicated Patel had been in prolonged contact with Mrs McLeish's blood-soaked body and acrylic fibres from her cardigan had been found on several parts of his anatomy.

In his defence Patel stated that he had been punched unconscious when he entered the twelfth-storey flat and that false evidence had been planted on him. It was his claim that he had been framed by the real killer and that he was just coming to his senses when the visitors had arrived.

The jury took over five hours to reach a unanimous verdict that Patel was solely responsible for the murder and sexual assault in the Preston tower block. As he was led down the steps from the dock flanked by two prison officers, he voiced his innocence of the crime. He was being taken away to begin the life sentence imposed upon him by Mr Justice Hodgson.

MYSTERY OF IMRAAN VOHRA
KILLER SOLVED

Preston folk were horrified in July 1985 by news of the killing of Imraan Vohra, aged nine, a pupil at Frenchwood Primary School who lived in James Street. He was last seen alive after school on the second Thursday afternoon of July. By 9 o'clock that night he had not returned home and his worried parents reported him missing.

A massive police search was undertaken for the Asian boy, with over 150 members of Preston's Muslim Society joining the search of nearby parklands. Mounted police and dog handlers were called in and an underwater team scoured the River Ribble.

He was last seen alive when he left Frenchwood Primary School on the Thursday afternoon.

Inset: Imraan Vohra.

The body was discovered in the wooded area besides the familiar forty-nine steps.

Early on the following Saturday morning two members of the Asian community found Imraan's lifeless, half-naked body in undergrowth on Avenham Park. His body was lying face upwards, around 100 yards from the Tram Bridge, near the area known locally as the forty-nine steps.

An immediate murder enquiry was launched to find the person responsible for the rape and killing. Marks on the schoolboy's neck suggested that he had been strangled with something thinner than a tie, possibly string or cable.

The police were anxious to interview all the visitors to the park on what had been a drizzly Thursday afternoon. There were reports of a stranger being seen around the school gates on the afternoon that Imraan died. He was described as 5 feet 10 inches tall, slim, with straight collar-length hair parted to the left.

Police investigations looked at different possibilities, considering whether he knew his killer and walked to the park willingly, or was lured to the scene by a stranger. Whoever strangled Imraan was to elude the police for many years. The case was never laid to rest, with his father Ismail often making desperate pleas to solve the mystery.

It was almost a quarter of a century before the identity of his killer was finally revealed. It was announced in September 2009 that the murderer was Robert David Morley, a known petty thief and fraudster who was aged forty-nine at the time of killing. A father of seven originally from London, Morley had lived in Preston from 1979, occupying an apartment in Lancaster House from 1983 until 1987. Latest advances in DNA technology meant that a DNA profile of the killer was matched with that of a close relative of Morley, the conclusion being drawn that the chances of the killer being anyone else was at least a billion to one. Morley, who had later moved to Essex, died from lung cancer in 1997 aged sixty-two.

Lancaster House, where killer Robert Morley had lived, was demolished in March 2004 along with the neighbouring York House.

CHRIST CHURCH STREET TRIPLE KILLING

On the first Monday of March 1987 the Preston fire brigade set off to attend a fire in Christ Church Street, Preston, shortly before 10 o'clock in the evening. After battling their way through the terraced house they came across the bodies of three men. It was obvious from the state of the victims that a terrible slaughter had taken place.

The outcome in July 1987 was the trial at Preston Crown Court of Mahmood Hussain, accused of the murder of Peter Mosley, aged twenty-one, Tahir Iqubul, aged twenty-one, and Ejaz Yousaf, aged twenty-three, at their fire ravaged lodgings. The prosecution claimed that the powerfully built Hussain had murdered Peter Morley in a row over a girlfriend, and then slaughtered the other two in cold blood to stop them identifying him as Morley's killer.

Hussain and Morley had been fellow students at Thames Polytechnic and Hussain had been in a stormy relationship with Dionne Gonga, aged twenty-one, a fellow student. When she tired of his possessive and jealous nature she turned her attention to Morley. Hussain had been enraged by the developing relationship between the couple and on one occasion struck both of them after finding them together.

When Hussain found out she had been to Preston to see Morley he was furious. Hiring a car, he set off for Preston, armed with a stolen knife and a gallon of paraffin. He was allowed entry to the Christ Church Street house by Tahir Iqubul, who showed him to Morley's room. At first Morley would not allow him in the room, but later relented and they discussed Dionne, with Morley insisting he would continue to see the girl. This clearly outraged Hussain, who, when Morley turned away from him, stabbed him in the back. As Morley collapsed to the floor Hussain stabbed him repeatedly with his 10-inch-long blade.

Hussain then lured Tahir upstairs and when he reached the door of Morley's room he was also stabbed several times and left for dead. Ejaz, who was in the next room, was alerted by the commotion and cries of Tahir and ran downstairs in a blind panic. Hussain followed hastily behind him and stabbed him in the back.

Leaving the house shortly after his killing spree, Hussain returned minutes later and poured paraffin over each body before setting them ablaze. He then started several other fires and took some cash and credit cards in the hope of making it look like a robbery gone wrong.

He then motored back to Birmingham where he covered his tracks by burning his gloves and bloodstained clothes, dumping the knife and the paraffin container. Along with his nephew, he then went to London, asking his nephew to say they had been together the previous day, if anyone should ask.

When the police interviewed Hussain he gave the false alibi, but there were discrepancies in his story and eventually he admitted the killing and the manner in which he had acted. Mr Justice Steyn sentenced Hussain to life imprisonment on each

Left: Christ Church Street in Preston where the killings took place.

Below: Victims of a cruel killer.

Mahmood Hussain's victims

Tahir Iqubal   **Ejaz Yousaf**   **Peter Mosley**

of the three counts of murder, with a recommendation that he served at least twenty years. Hussain showed little emotion as he was led away.

It was revealed later that a fourth resident of the ill-fated house, a woman, aged twenty-seven, who was staying with family at Hutton on the night of the tragedy, might well have been a fourth victim.

After three failed attempts to secure his freedom Mahmood Hussain was finally released in October 2010, after spending seven years in an open prison, much to the despair of the families of the victims.

HOSTAGES AT THE NATWEST BANK

The present-day Fishers public house was a familiar bank on Fishergate from late 1931 until 1991. Originally the County Bank, it was the premises of the National Westminster Bank before they moved their banking business to newly built premises. After a spell as the Wall Street public house it became the Fishers.

Those premises on the site of the Old Legs of Man public house will forever be associated with the events of mid-September 1988 when an armed robbery took place and over sixty bank staff were held hostage.

On the second Wednesday of September 1988 Roger Ball, the bank manager, left the bank shortly after 6 o'clock in the evening and walked towards his Ford Sierra, parked at a nearby car park. Next to his car was a small red van and he noticed one of his car tyres was deflated. As he made his way to his car boot the van doors sprang open and two balaclava-clad men jumped out. They grabbed him and forced him face down into the van, tying him up, placing a hood over his head and removing his keys from his grasp.

His abductors then drove to a car park at Morecambe Golf Club where he was told to telephone his wife, Jean, and daughter, Vanessa, aged thirteen, and inform them of the situation. The men then drove to Mr Ball's family home in Morecambe where the kidnappers explained their intention of robbing the bank, having made themselves familiar with the layout and staffing levels.

At 4 o'clock in the morning the three hostages, bound, gagged and hooded, were taken in the boots of two cars to an empty shop off Fishergate. Some five hours later Mr Ball was ordered to go to the bank and inform the sixty-two staff that a robbery was about to take place and that they must assemble in the vaults.

Half an hour later Mr Ball let the armed robbers into the bank and holding the staff at gunpoint, they cleared the vaults of money before locking the staff inside. The gang then calmly made their getaway, taking the cash through the front doors of the bank on Fishergate.

The police became aware of the incident when Mrs Ball managed to alert a passer-by as she broke a window in the shop where she and her daughter were being held hostage. Armed police arrived at the bank shortly before 10 o'clock and twenty police marksmen ringed the four-storey building, with another 100 police officers standing by.

Police negotiators were called in but when no contact was made by noon, a police firearms team entered the bank using a set of spare keys. Inside they found the hostages unharmed and learnt that the gang and the money had long since departed.

With £528,000 stolen, kidnapping and hostage taking, painstaking investigations got underway immediately to identify the members of the ruthless gang, who it was thought came from Merseyside. A significant breakthrough came eight weeks after the raid when James Gibson, aged twenty-three, was the victim of a gangster-style killing. He was blasted with a shotgun just a 100 yards from his home in Walton, Liverpool. His killer was seen running to a getaway car that sped away in the night. When police later searched the home of Gibson and found cash they believed was from the NatWest raid they turned their attention to his mate Leonard Newsham, who was watched by detectives.

After being interviewed by police at Preston he was kept under surveillance and was watched as he went into the grounds of Fazackerley Hospital. After seeing Newsham digging up a package the police pounced and almost £12,000 in bank notes were seized, which were later identified as being part of the NatWest haul. This development led to a further search of the grounds and the discovery of another package containing two balaclavas that matched fibres found in the getaway vehicles.

The police believed six men were involved in the crime and Newsham became terrified of similar retribution, he and Gibson having been two members of the gang with the least authority and required to take the greatest risks.

In late November 1989 Leonard Newsham, aged twenty-four, appeared at Preston Crown Court on charges of robbery, kidnapping and false imprisonment. The details of the charges were outlined on the first day by prosecutor Brian Leveson with claims that Newsham, who pleaded not guilty, and Gibson played leading roles in the operation carried out with military precision.

With the evidence obviously stacked against him, Newsham dramatically changed his plea to guilty on all counts after discussions between defence and prosecution lawyers. Judge Schiemann then ordered the jury to return guilty verdicts and Newsham was sentenced to thirteen years' imprisonment.

The NatWest Bank on Fishergate.

The original Preston Sessions House, opened in 1903, where the NatWest Bank robbery trial took place in 1989. The Preston Crown Court was established there in 1975 prior to the building of the present-day Preston Crown Court on Ringway in 1995.

A couple of years later three people were charged with handling proceeds of the robbery when police carried out a dawn raid on a home in Fleetwood and recovered £140,000. This led to John Hay, aged forty-four, Desmond Penny, aged twenty-two, and Newsham's girlfriend Sharon Crawford, aged twenty-two, appearing at Preston Crown Court after admitting handling cash and travellers cheques valued at over £500,000. They had carried out an elaborate plot to divert the proceeds of the robbery to bank accounts in Ireland. Hay, who was seen as central to the operation, was jailed for four years, Crawford was sentenced to six months in prison and Penny received a twelve-month suspended sentence, which were handed out by Judge Robert Brown.

Upon his release Hay went to America and in 1995 he appeared in court in Nevada accused of trying to smuggle cocaine into the United Kingdom. Found guilty, he was sentenced to a maximum twenty-five years in jail. As for Newsham, who was due for release in November 1997, he committed an armed robbery while on home leave from Sudbury prison near Derby. Appearing at Liverpool Crown Court in late September 1997, along with his alleged accomplice Kevin Booth, he was found guilty of a terrifying raid on a family in Foxwood, West Derby. Judge Clarke described him as a professional criminal and sentenced him to twelve more years in prison.

ACKNOWLEDGEMENTS

I must acknowledge the help given to me by the staff of the Harris Community Library in Preston, who willingly assist as I delve into their archives. My appreciation also goes to the newspaper reporters of the past who, in chronicling the events of their day, left a valuable legacy. The *Lancashire Post, Preston Guardian, Preston Chronicle, Preston Pilot* and *Preston Herald* all provided information from their publications. Their accounts and my research into the court archives have made this book possible.

Besides my own collection of images/illustrations, I would like to thank the *Lancashire Post* for permission to use images that are contacted with my Court Archives features, or are nowadays stored in the Preston Digital Archive. Also, my thanks go to Richard H. Parker, the creator of the PDA, for use of images from that source, and to Mike Hill, Communities Editor of the *Lancashire Post*, who is ever helpful in my research and so enthusiastic with regards to local history.

My thanks also to Pat Crook for cheerfully checking my manuscript and putting her literary skills at my disposal once again.

ABOUT THE AUTHOR

Keith Johnson is Preston born and bred. His previous works include the bestselling Chilling True Tales series of books featuring Preston, Lancashire and London, and the popular *People of Old Preston, Preston Remembered, Preston Through Time, Preston in the 1960s, Secret Preston, Preston in 50 Buildings, Preston History Tour, Preston at Work, A–Z of Preston, Now That's What I Call Preston* and *Preston Military Heritage* books. For over fifteen years he has contributed numerous feature articles on local history to the *Lancashire Post*, and since 2011 has written a weekly Court Archive for the *LP Retro* magazine.

Keith was educated at St Augustine's Boys' School in Preston prior to attending Harris College where he gained his qualifications for a career in engineering, spending forty years working for the printing press manufacturer Goss.